STRATEGIES OF OPTIMISM

Vera Peiffer was born near Cologne in Germany. At University she studied German, English Literature and Linguistics, and in 1981 she moved to Britain where she obtained a BA in Psychology. She became interested in hypnotherapy and completed a diploma at the Hypnothink Foundation. She followed this with a further diploma in analytical hypnotherapy at the Hypnotherapy Centre in Bournemouth.

Vera now runs a private practice as an analytical hypno-therapist-psychoanalyst in Ealing, West London. She also teaches stress management at the London Business School and is a member of the International Association of Hypno-Analysts in Bournemouth.

By the same author
POSITIVE THINKING

STRATEGIES
OF OPTIMISM

A PRACTICAL GUIDE TO PERSONAL DEVELOPMENT

Vera Peiffer

E L E M E N T   B O O K S

© Vera Peiffer 1990
First published in Great Britain in 1990 by
Element Books Limited
Longmead, Shaftesbury, Dorset

Cover illustration by Jennie Smith
Designed by Max Fairbrother

Typeset by Input Typesetting, London
Printed and Bound in Great Britain
by Billings Ltd, Hylton Road, Worcester

British Library Cataloguing in Publication Data
Peiffer, Vera
Strategies of optimism : a practical guide to personal development.
1. Self-development
I. Title

ISBN 1-85230-143-0

For Vivien van Hoof

People are always blaming their circumstances for what they are. I don't believe in circumstances. The people who get on in this world are the people who get up and look for the circumstances they want, and if they can't find them, make them.

G. B. SHAW
Mrs Warren's Profession

CONTENTS

PART I

1. ARE WE FREE AGENTS OR DETERMINED?

IN THE early hours of 9th January 1800, in the village of Saint-Sernin in southern France, the tanner was woken up by strange noises coming from his terraced garden. It was still quite dark outside, so that when he peered out of his window he could only just make out a figure rooting around in one of his vegetable patches. The tanner decided to investigate further and, having put on some clothes, silently entered the garden. Cautiously he stole closer to the intruder who was so intent on digging for vegetables, that the tanner could grab him without much of a struggle. When he took a closer look at his captive he was surprised to see that the intruder was a mere boy, short in stature and naked except for an old shirt that hung in shreds from his under-nourished body. The boy could not speak, and the only sounds he made were weird cries. Although he walked erect and his body was human, his movements, gestures and behaviour suggested an animal.

The appearance and capture of Victor, as the boy was later called, created an immediate sensation in the quiet little village of Saint-Sernin. Word spread rapidly that a wild boy had been caught who looked as if he had spent years living rough.

At the time he was found, Victor was about twelve years old. His body was covered with scars and he displayed the behaviour of an animal. He was perfectly indifferent to heat

or cold, had no awareness of himself as a person, relieved
himself wherever he sat or stood and would not eat anything
unless he had smelled it first. He showed great skill at climb-
ing trees and preferred a diet of roots and wild berries. When
he was offered a choice of meat, bread, apples, pears, grapes,
potatoes and parsnips, he picked the potatoes which seemed
familiar to him and tossed them into the fire. Later he would
pick the potatoes, still half-raw, out of the live coals with his
bare hands and, to the horror of the onlookers, begin to eat
them roasting hot. It proved impossible to persuade him to
wait until they had cooled off. Whenever Victor found himself
with more food than he could eat, he buried the leftovers in
the garden, just like an animal who stores food for a later
time.

The sensational discovery of the 'wild boy of Aveyron' was
soon to become a matter of national importance. The news
spread all the way to Paris where Jean Itard, a young surgeon
at the Institute for Deaf Mutes, took an interest in the boy.
For five years, Itard worked with the boy to prove that Victor's
mind could be awakened; that he was not an idiot, only
retarded in his development because he had been cut off from
human society for so long.

Jean Itard's dedication to Victor's development was only
partly motivated by compassion for the unfortunate child.
Victor's socialisation and humanisation was also desirable
because it would help prove Itard's point in a scientific contro-
versy: that Victor was asocial not because of a birth defect in
his mental make-up but because of the lack of human society
during his years in the wild. Itard was of the opinion that
man is not 'born' but 'constructed'. He believed that we are
born with empty heads and that it is our environment that
forms us rather than our personality or genetic heredity. The
discovery of Victor presented an opportunity for Itard to demonstrate the accuracy of his thesis. If he succeeded in educat-
ing Victor so as to make him resemble a normal human being
he could silence his opponents who claimed that wild children
were mentally retarded from birth and therefore abandoned
by their parents, rather than being retarded *because* of their
abandonment.

During Itard's five-year training programme, Victor progressed considerably. Although he never learnt to speak more

than a few words, he acquired basic reading skills and learnt to convey simple ideas by writing. His emotional life became richer and he showed genuine affection for Itard and his housekeeper, Madame Guérin, who became a foster-mother to the boy. Victor also learnt to appreciate different temperatures, began to enjoy the comforts of a warm bath and would no longer eat potatoes unless they were properly cooked.

After initial encouraging improvements, however, Victor's development came to a standstill. Although Victor could hear, his inability to learn to speak turned out to be the main impediment to further education. Also, his emotional development was blocked by his violent and unsatisfied sexual desires and the impossibility of channelling them towards a satisfactory goal. And yet, considering Victor's behaviour and state of mind at the beginning of his education, Itard had worked a miracle with the boy.

So who had been right, Itard or his opponents? Was Victor's development retarded because he had been isolated from human society or had he been born mentally retarded?

Even though Victor's case is well-documented from the time he was found, it is difficult to assess the outcome accurately. Nothing is known about his early childhood. There is evidence that he had lived in the mountains for five to six years when he was found at the age of approximately twelve, but where he lived before that time remains a mystery. It is therefore impossible to determine what his original mental capacity was.

There are many more cases of children that have been brought up in near total isolation, raised in captivity in dark rooms for years on end, hidden away from the outside world because they were illegitimate or unwanted, with just the barest of human contact. As their tragic fates come to light and they are finally released from their prisons, all these children show that their mental and physical development has suffered considerably. They often appear younger than their age, their physical maturation having been stunted by lack of food or the inability to metabolise the food properly under their restrictive conditions. Many of these children never manage to learn to walk. Their mental development is mostly grossly retarded, speech does not usually develop and the children have great difficulties relating to other people.

In some instances, infants were kept in isolation for scientific purposes. Frederick the Second, the Holy Roman Emperor, experimented with infants tended by nurses who had strict orders to feed the babies well but never to pet or kiss them or laugh or speak with them. By depriving the children of a speech model, the Emperor hoped to find the oldest language of mankind which he expected these children to start speaking after a while. The experiment failed: all the children died. The mere physical presence of the nurses had not been enough to keep them alive. The lack of emotional warmth not only prevented normal mental development but even basic physical survival.

Human development, then, is dependent on a supportive environment that helps nourish the first manifestations of mental growth, but development also depends on our biological structure. Genetic make-up and inherited biological traits can influence the extent to which we progress. Untreated shortsightedness can hinder mental development considerably, as can an undiscovered hearing problem. A shy and physically weak child may find it difficult to cope at a school where the most important thing is to be good at sports, and this can lead to loss of self-confidence and withdrawal from others.

It is not really a question of whether it is our social environment *or* our genetic heredity that makes us what we are; it is rather a combination of both aspects that determines how we develop initially. We are born with a certain disposition, certain personality traits and a unique genetic make-up. In the beginning, we are very dependent on our immediate environment for shelter and support. We have to rely on our parents to look after us and provide for us. Our lives are ruled by what our parents think and believe, what they consider to be right or wrong.

As we grow up, the influence our environment exerts on us multiplies.

We encounter new situations which differ from the familiar pattern; school begins, teachers make new demands on us, we have to learn to fit in with other children, to compete and to cooperate. We start reading books and magazines, and once we have acquired reading skills we are exposed to a myriad of stimuli. It becomes virtually impossible *not* to read because we are surrounded by written material in the form of advertisement posters, stickers and notices, newspapers and magazines.

Most of the time there is not a lot we can do about our biological make-up or the fact that problems arise in our environment. We have to learn to live with the realisation that we have, for example, short legs and will never make it as a model, and we equally have to accept that we failed to get into college or that we have just been made redundant. And yet, within the constraints of environment and biology we are free to make choices. For every difficulty we encounter in life there are several solutions. To believe that we are author of our own destiny does not deny that we may be severely restricted by circumstances, but if we are unhappy with our circumstances we have the freedom to go and seek out more favourable conditions. We have always at least one other option besides self-pity.

2. INDIVIDUAL AND SOCIETY

LET us take a closer look at the constraints that are imposed on us by our environment. It would be foolhardy to assume that we can overrule these constraints without some sort of consequences. A confirmed nudist cannot get on the morning train stark naked and travel to work without being picked up by the police at some stage of his journey. If, however, it was customary to travel nude, we might witness a scene where a weird gentleman in a pinstriped suit and a bowler hat was led away by men in white coats.

Our freedom of choice and our freedom to develop in whatever direction we wish is certainly limited by the society we live in. For one thing we cannot choose what we don't know about. If we have never heard of the profession of chiropody,

we will not have the option of entering it. The problem of
ignorance is not so great in modern times; the mass media
ensure that news and information is available to everyone.
This has not always been so. A few hundred years ago not
everyone could read, certain professions were reserved for
people of wealth and standing, and it was customary for the
son to follow in the father's professional footsteps and the
daughter to get married as early as possible and have children.
Organisations and institutions, written and unwritten rules
and regulations channel development in particular ways. Our
parents and later our teachers introduce us to the fundamental
values of society. As children, we are initially utterly dependent on all these teachings, simply because we regard our
parents as gods who are always right and whose love is essential for our physical and emotional survival. Even though
children begin to rebel once their critical faculties start developing, their emotional needs still tie them to their parents and
make them dependent on the parents' attitudes and opinions.
The longer you spend with a person, the more likely it is that
you adopt their values. In this way, a child's picture of the
world is not entirely his own creation but rather a mixture of
what adults have taught him and his own fantasies about the
things he still does not understand. The church used to have
and often still has enormous power over our conception of
what is right and what is wrong, and those readers who have
been brought up in a strict religious tradition will be able to
confirm how their perception of the world was shaped by
teachings based on their particular religion.

Even though we perceive ourselves as individuals, with our
own personal problems, hopes and aspirations, we are at the
same time members of the society and culture we live in. We
are in constant contact, voluntarily or involuntarily, with other
people who have *their* personal problems, hopes and aspirations. This ongoing necessity to interact with others obliges
us to learn to understand ourselves and others in order to
create a positive social environment in which we feel happy
and accepted. This, as we all know, is no mean feat. We have
to learn to predict other people's reactions to our own actions
and, if necessary, modify our behaviour accordingly. Once
little Harry has grasped that mum has a fit every time he
walks over the living room carpet in his muddy wellies, he

will make use of this newly acquired knowledge by either hiding to avoid her wrath next time he leaves his footprints all over the Axminster, or, if his mother is lucky, by taking off his boots before he enters the living room.

During childhood we learn a great number of things via reward and punishment. We are praised when we behave in a quiet and well-mannered way at Auntie Maude's, and we get hissed at when we comment on the fact that Uncle Paul is going bald or marvel aloud at granny's ability to take her teeth out at night.

Some of our social behaviour we are taught by parents and teachers, other norms we learn by observing others and imitating them if the outcome seems rewarding. This tendency to learn by copying was demonstrated in an experiment where three groups of pre-school children were shown a film about an adult beating up a large doll. The first group saw an ending where the adult was rewarded for his behaviour by another adult, the second group saw the adult punished, and the third group saw an indifferent ending where the observing adult's behaviour remained neutral. When the children were then encouraged to play with a life-size doll, the first and third group kicked and thumped the doll, whereas the second group who had seen this behaviour punished were obviously holding back. When, however, all children were promised chocolate if they kicked the doll, the second group's resistance dwindled within seconds. . .

Outside stimuli and adult role models, together with our personality make-up and all our experiences in life so far, will result in us forming a model of the world in our heads, a mental picture of how we assume the world around us works. The son of a banker may think of bankers as generally helpful people, whereas someone whose only experience of bankers is that of receiving unpleasant letters may look at bankers as enemies. A little boy who is constantly humiliated by his mother may develop a negative image of women and in later life react with secret or open satisfaction when he reads about violence against women.

Our experiences will determine how we perceive the world around us. This point is illustrated quite clearly by the parable of the three blind men who are all asked to describe what an elephant looks like. Depending on which part of the elephant they are touching, they all deliver vastly different accounts so that each of them seems to be describing an entirely different animal. None of them sees the elephant as it actually is, yet each one is sure that he is right.

As we grow up we not only form an image of the world around us in our minds, we also form an image of our self. The reflections we get from others serve as feedback, the way others react to us functions as a mirror in which we see ourselves. When a child's attempts to communicate are met with indifference or impatience, the child understands this reaction as a personal rebuke, as a message that means, 'You are not worth listening to.' This self-image imprinted in us early on by parents and teachers will later be accepted by us as our self.

One of the preconditions for development is knowing how you feel. Children often have to deny their negative feelings in order to keep their parents' love. In this way, parents can impose on a child their views of her feelings. When Jennie hits her little brother and her parents comment that surely she does not want to hurt him, Jennie may feel obliged to agree, although she *is* angry and she *wants* to hurt him because he has annoyed her. But as her anger is obviously not acceptable to her parents she conforms to their version of reality and makes it her own, thus denying her angry feelings and feeling guilty about them every time they recur.

But we are not just passive recipients of the influences acting upon us. Society influences us, but in return we also influence society. There is always a two-way interaction between ourselves and the people we relate to. A further point to note is that not only can we influence others but we can also influence ourselves. We have the ability to construct our own reality, but that means taking responsibility for the choices we make. Many people fear this freedom of choice and prefer to stick to convention or fashion or ideologies. The price they pay for not creating their own reality is that they don't run their own life but allow someone else to run it for them. Ultimately, they are not living their own life but someone else's; they shape themselves into how they think they 'should' be, but aren't. It is no good, for example, trying to be a working mother just because this is the fashion at the moment, when really you would like nothing better than to stay at home with the kids.

In order to grow and develop we have to become acquainted with our own needs and feelings and be open to explore new experiences. It takes courage to extend one's boundaries, but it is well worth it as it leads to a more fulfilling life by enabling us to reach our full potential.

3. DEVELOPMENT AS AN ONGOING PROCESS

WHEN we speak of development, we often think of physical development, for example when a baby gains weight, cuts its first teeth and eventually begins to lose its baby looks. As the child gets older the entire physical frame gradually transforms, and later physical attributes of puberty emerge. Once the bones have reached their final length, growth in height comes to a standstill. After this stage, development turns retrogressive and physical faculties eventually deteriorate after the peak of maturation has been reached.

But development also takes place on the mental side. We are quite aware of this fact during the initial stages of early childhood when the baby learns to walk and talk, when a young child learns to read and write and even later when a student studies a particular subject at university or an apprentice acquires new skills at his workplace. What we tend to notice less is development on the social level such as the acquisition of social graces, the ability to form friendships, the ability to fill a variety of role positions, for example switching from being a husband to being a father, and the ability to master a variety of problems like coping with stress, illness, financial worries and interpersonal upheavals.

All the developmental steps that are linked to education we take more or less for granted because they are shared by most people. Schooling is compulsory to a certain age and higher education is more likely to secure a good professional position, and subsequently we subject ourselves to the learning process more or less happily, according to our personality and disposition. But schooling often takes second place in a young person's life, and this is not really surprising when you think of all the fundamental physical and emotional changes that take place during puberty. Budding sexual desires coupled with curiosity, shyness and inexperience leave you with the energy of a wet lettuce to pursue subjects like the Battle of Trafalgar or French irregular verbs. When you are busy finding out about yourself, your body and your relationship to others, in other words, when you are on your way to becoming an adult, school is at best an unwelcome interruption. Bluestockings are often youngsters who are unsuccessful or fearful of forming relationships and who therefore bury themselves in their textbooks.

By the time we leave school or university we have spent between ten and fifteen years improving our knowledge and obtaining qualifications for a future job, only to find that theoretical knowledge does not immediately translate into practical know-how when it comes to applying what we have learnt. The learning process must go on, this time based on daily experience. But finally we reach the stage where we have come to grips with the job and are able to master irregularities and problems reasonably well, where we can sit back and enjoy the fact that we have made it professionally, and this is a truly uplifting feeling.

Unfortunately it is at this point where learning and therefore development often comes to a halt. After a few years, routine sets in and we begin to lose the ability and even the desire to seek out new areas and improve on our abilities. Life becomes the nine-to-five workday with dinner in front of the television in the evening or the fourteen-hour-day with the kids and sleeping in front of the television. We have 'settled down', our lives are beginning to run along a particular track and when we get to a junction we go for the easy option. We do not tackle any more new things except the occasional promotion or change of job, but personally we function along the same old lines until we are pensioned off. As a consequence we become rigid and less skilful at solving problems, and the more we avoid new and possibly difficult situations the less practice we get at mastering them and the less confidence we have to attempt any more new situations. This is a problem many women who have left their jobs to bring up children face when they find themselves worried and unnerved at the prospect of seeking employment again. The same is true for people who live for their work. They lose contact with the outside world, and have no other interests or resources. Once they retire, these people are more prone to depression and early death than those who have built up interesting pastimes over the years. At first sight, it may appear the safer option to avoid involvement in new situations, but in the long run you are losing out on a lot of fun and excitement.

For a long time, psychologists were inclined to believe that there is a critical period of time within which a child's mental and social development must be achieved. It was thought that it was impossible for the child to make up for missed experiences or to recover from trauma once it had passed the age of six. We now know that this sort of view can turn into a self-fulfilling prophecy: because it is deemed impossible to socialise deprived children once they are over a certain age, nobody attempts to help them, and therefore these children never improve, which then confirms the theory that there is no possibility of improvement after the age of six.

It is of course quite true that traumatic events in early childhood have an effect on a person, but this does not mean that a trauma has to affect the rest of that person's life. Just because we have missed out on love and affection when we were little does not mean we cannot secure it for ourselves when we are grown up; just because we have been unhappy and dejected as children does not mean we cannot grow up to be happy adults. Getting over traumatic events can be difficult, and in some cases outside help is needed, but it nevertheless can be achieved. There are many cases where people from the most abject backgrounds managed to get themselves sorted out and led a happy and successful life later on.

The means of self-fulfilment and contentment lie in our own hands. It takes courage to work towards one's own happiness because it means taking the risk of trying new ways and learning more about oneself and one's feelings, and it takes determination to persevere on a new way and not give up at the sight of the first obstacle. Changes don't usually come about suddenly, so we have enough time to adapt gradually to them as they happen. Changes are going on around us all the time and we have to adjust to them, so why not make those changes benefit us? We can set our own personal goals and work towards them. This will ensure that we continue to grow and progress continuously, way beyond any biological deadlines.

4. OPTIMISM VERSUS PESSIMISM

WHEN you read the newspapers these days you may well think that there is little reason to be optimistic. Wars and upheaval everywhere; revolts that leave thousands dead; chaos produced by strikes that are carried out by desperate people; inner city violence where muggings, hold-ups, break-ins and rape occur daily; rising inflation and interest rates that create havoc for so many families; progressive destruction of the environment with irreparable damage to forests, water and atmosphere, and the threatened or already accomplished extinction of so much wildlife. Surely only an ignorant or uncaring person or someone with a less than serious disposition can contemplate all these events and still be hopeful!

It appears that bad news, unlike good news, travels fast indeed. It is also treated as more newsworthy than any positive news there may be. Consider the daily diet of newspapers, television and radio. Their news sections are so often filled with the problems of the world, they virtually live on trouble, crises and catastrophes. Why is it that generally only negative events are reported? After a barrage of television news of death, terror and violence we are finally informed that some zoo has managed to produce a baby Panda bear, presumably in the hope that this tinsel of good news will lighten the enormous burden of negative news.

This negative selection we are often exposed to by the media makes us forget that, indeed, this *is* a selection. Someone has picked out certain items from a vast number of events that have occurred in the world that day – and then presents them as 'reality'. But even the few chosen events that are deemed important enough to be broadcast are clipped down to a few minutes of commentary and some short film sequences, so we are left with an even narrower window through which to assess the situation.

It would be interesting to see what happened if one day an editor decided to broadcast only good news, to deliberately emphasise only the positive things that are going on in the world, how people get together to plant trees or restore old buildings; how relationships between countries are getting better; how nations or companies or individuals master problems, demonstrating the solutions they have found so that everyone can learn from them. And only a few seconds at the end about violence and killings. . . I'm sure a lot of people would feel cheated. Surely this cannot be all! Surely there must be some more important news! Isn't it odd, though, that we never ask ourselves these same questions when we hear about all the misery in the world?

Media coverage these days seems to suggest that problems are on the increase. But are they really? Or is it just the media reports about these problems that are on the increase? In recent years, for example, there have been a growing number of articles and programmes on topics such as child abuse and battered women. These are serious issues that deserve to be discussed, and media coverage plays a main role in increasing awareness by bringing them to public attention, but this does not mean that more children are abused now than were 20 years ago. It only means that, because of greater awareness and therefore greater openness about the problem, more people come forward and report incidents which in turn leads to more extensive media coverage.

The media fulfil an important function in that they help unveil taboo subjects, and only by looking at a problem can we proceed to seek a solution, but we still have to bear in mind that the media cannot claim to reflect reality in its entirety and that, just because we suddenly read a lot about a certain problem, it does not mean that that problem is getting worse. It just means that we are hearing more about it.

This increased awareness has its price, though. We are beginning to feel out of control, and with every news round we feel more depressed and discouraged. Although consciously we can try and ignore the negative information, subconsciously we are affected. Negative images produce negative feelings, whether we want it or not (see also my book *Positive Thinking*).

Just as the negative information in the news bulletin distorts reality, so does the display of mental and physical strength in films. If we measure ourselves against the heroes of the films we watch, we will find ourselves sadly lacking, and if we listen to all the awful news we feel doubly incapable of coping.

In order to avoid falling into that trap it is important to bear in mind that it is *we* who are the reality and it is therefore *we* who have to be the measure of competence, not some illusory hero on television. We have a choice of how much we want to expose ourselves to negative influences. Is it really necessary to listen to the news on the radio, read a newspaper *and* watch the news bulletin on television in the evening? It is laudable to want to be informed, but surely there is no need to brainwash yourself into a negative frame of mind!

Equally, why do we find it so easy to criticise and so very difficult to praise? It seems that we have an established pattern of negative thinking, looking out for the 'downers'. Pessimism seems so safe: you can always be sure that something is going to go wrong sometime. Many people seem to be afraid of being optimistic. It is almost like a superstition that if you are too happy you are asking for disaster.

The problem with negative thinking of course is that it works as a self-fulfilling prophecy. Because you think negatively you are tense, nervous, moody and not at your best. If a difficult situation arises you are therefore less likely to cope adequately than someone who is in a positive frame of mind. Because you cope badly you find your premonitions of impending disaster confirmed and your negative thinking reinforced, and so the vicious circle is established.

Luckily, there is no need for you to go through life in this negative manner because the system works just as well the other way round. We are aware that life is neither always wonderful nor always miserable. The truth may lie somewhere in the middle, and we can tip the balance in our favour by consciously choosing to look at the bright side.

This doesn't mean that we should ignore difficulties or avoid problems, on the contrary. Running away from problems is useless because they will just run after you. What we need to do is to turn around and take a good look at what is bothering or frightening us, and then take appropriate action to deal with it. If we have a pessimistic attitude we will be doubtful as to whether it is worth solving the problem, whereas if we are optimistic, we will be prepared to tackle it. When you look back at all the improvements that have been achieved over the years concerning medicine, engineering and technology, you are looking at achievements by optimists who believed that there had to be a solution to the problems they encountered – and they went to look for that solution. A pessimist would have just given up and never discovered the answer. When we think of the pollution that is being produced by industry, jeopardising our environment, and all the endangered species that are being killed for profit, we could easily despair and resign ourselves to the fact that we have gone too far in ruining our planet and that there is nothing we can do about it any more. But one optimist decided that it was not too late to get started on a rescue mission and set up an organisation like Greenpeace, the World Wild Life Fund or Amnesty International. This optimist was joined by others who thought alike, and after a while there are large organisations which would become influential and have clout with governments. Granted, progress is slow, but it is gradually becoming more visible. It takes time to instigate change in people's attitudes and behaviour, and we often get impatient because we want to see results quickly.

Optimism is the belief that it is worthwhile to make an effort; optimism is the hope that a positive outcome can be achieved, in spite of any obstacles that might bar the way. It takes courage to be optimistic but it is our only option if we want to succeed and avoid the dead-end street of resignation and negativity.

5. SOME FAIRY TALES AND THEIR SEQUELS

I DON'T know if you remember those old fairy tales, whether they were ever read to you at bedtime to help you go to sleep. To my mind, if there is one sure antidote to untroubled and restful sleep, it is fairy tales. Think about the plots: all you ever hear about is harrassed heroes who have to fight giants or man-eating wolves or evil sorcerers in order to live happily ever after; or they are required to answer silly questions unless they want their heads chopped off, and they had only come to woo a beautiful princess. I ask you, do you find that relaxing? You might as well tell your kids to go and watch a horror movie on TV! Why does the princess have to allow a horrible little frog onto her pillow when everyone knows that it is unhygienic to have animals in your bed? Why does Cinderella have to go through the rigmarole of getting home by midnight? If she is allowed out in a low-cut evening dress, surely she is old enough to decide for herself when she has had enough dancing and drinking champagne or whatever it is they serve in fairy tale castles.

Fairy tales are full of hassles and obstacles for their heroes who are often children or young adults. Luckily the stories usually have a happy ending where the good are rewarded and the bad punished. But have you ever wondered what would have happened had our heroes found themselves in a similar situation later on in life? Would they have matured and acquired further knowledge, skill and common sense? Assuming that they had progressed in their personal development in the meantime, how would they now tackle life's ups and downs? Let us look at some of those fairy tales and speculate on their possible sequels.

LITTLE RED RIDING-HOOD

The story so far:

SOMEWHERE out in the countryside lives a single mother with her little girl whom she loves very much. One day she has a red riding-hood made for her, and as she insists her daughter wear it every day, the unfortunate child is soon addressed by everyone as Little Red Riding-Hood.

One day, Little Red Riding-Hood is sent to take some food to her sick grandmother who lives in another village. In order to get there Little Red Riding-Hood has to pass through a great big forest. She meets a big bad wolf who has every intention of making her his supper, but as there are some faggot-makers nearby he restrains himself for the time being. Instead, he starts chatting to Little Red Riding-Hood, complimenting her on her red cape, peering at the goodies in her basket and enquiring harmlessly where she is going. When he finds out that she is on her way to grandmamma, he suggests that they take different routes and see who arrives first. Little Red Riding-Hood agrees naïvely to this little game, but soon forgets about it as she dawdles along, picking poisonous mushrooms and chasing butterflies. When she finally gets to her grandmother's, the wolf has long arrived and made use of his advantage by eating the grandmother, donning her nightgown and cap and slipping into her bed to await Little Red Riding-Hood's arrival. When the girl enters her grandmother's bedroom, she is somewhat puzzled at the changes that have occurred to her dear grandmamma. She points out that grandma appears to have hairy pointed ears and great big eyes, but she is reassured in each case that this is all no cause for alarm and only a late side-effect of the pill. Only when the girl enquires about the exceptionally large teeth grandmother seems to have grown does the wolf reveal his true intention, gobble down Little Red Riding-Hood and fall asleep. His thunderous snores are overheard by a passing huntsman who enters the house to investigate. When he sees the wolf in drag he guesses what has happened and cuts open the wolf, thus freeing Little Red Riding-Hood and grandmother, who are both exhausted but unharmed thanks to the wolf's tardy digestion.

The sequel:

TWENTY years later, and Little Red Riding-Hood has grown up into an attractive young lady who has shed her red cape as well as her silly nickname and has instead acquired a little red sportscar. She has left her village and gone to a nearby town to become personal assistant to a managing director, making coffee, ringing up the service people to have the photocopier repaired once a week and correcting her boss's spelling mistakes. But she still sees her mother and is also in touch with her grandmother who refuses to go into an old people's home. However, the shock of the incident with the wolf has done nothing to improve grandmamma's health, and so, once again, Fiona sets out with a large carrier bag of delicatessen for grandmamma.

As she is whizzing down the motorway she notices a young wolf in an old Ford, shirt open to the navel and sporting a gold medallion on his hairy chest, trying to attract her attention. He is flashing his lights, driving along next to her car and generally making a thorough nuisance of himself; but as his car has only an 0.9 litre engine he doesn't manage to overtake our heroine and has to make do with the superior little smile she gives him in her rear view mirror.

Progress: Ameliorated financial circumstances enable you to drive a car that is fast enough to get you away from bothersome admirers.

But the young wolf decides to rise to the challenge and follows the girl in the sportscar. He manages to catch up with her at a petrol station, but keeps out of sight as she continues to her grandmother's house. As she gets involved in a chat with a neighbour, he slips into the house by the backdoor, drags the bewildered grandmother out of bed and, being vegetarian, locks her in the wardrobe. On arrival, Fiona is greatly surprised at finding a wolf in her grandmother's bed, wearing her nightcap and glasses, but she is not fooled by the animal's silly disguise.

> *Progress:* **Regular attendance of biology classes at school ensures correct discrimination between a wolf and a grandmother.**

Fiona threatens the wolf with legal action should he not reveal the whereabouts of her grandmother and then clear out immediately. When the wolf just laughs and tries to knock her about a bit, Fiona delivers a few well-placed karate chops to his neck which put the wolf out of action.

> *Progress:* **Knowing your rights is essential. Being able to defend them in times of crisis is even better.**

When she drags the wolf to the wardrobe to lock him up she finds her grandmother, frees her and calmly awaits the arrival of the police.

RUMPELSTILTSKIN

The story so far:

A POOR miller has a daughter who is not only very good-looking but also highly intelligent. The miller, himself not very bright, spends his days going around bragging about her and one day, when he has had a few too many, goes as far as telling the king of the land that his daughter can spin gold out of straw. This is an unfortunate move, since the king is not only unmarried but also greedy. He orders the girl to be brought before him, leads her to a chamber which is equipped with a spinning wheel and stacked to the ceiling with straw, and orders her to turn the straw into gold, threatening to have her executed if she fails. The girl hastens to assure him that she can do no such thing, but he refuses to listen and locks her in.

After spending some time thinking unfavourable thoughts about her father, who has landed her in this critical situation, the girl sits down in a corner and starts crying. All of a sudden the door opens and a peculiarly undersized chap comes hobbling in. He leers at her and promises to help her provided she parts with some of her jewellery. This the young girl gladly agrees to and hands him her necklace.

The next morning the king comes back and discovers to his delight that the straw has indeed been turned into gold, and he immediately begins to make further business plans. He leads the girl into an even larger room with straw, and again threatens her with death unless she delivers the gold by morning. Again, the girl is helped by the gnome who takes her ring in payment for his assistance.

But the king's greed is without limit. He orders the girl into an even bigger chamber and, eyeing her lustily, promises to make her queen once that particular job lot is done. Even though the miller's daughter is not certain that marrying the king is preferable to getting executed, she waits, hoping that the little man will be there to help once again. He is indeed, but by now she has exhausted her supply of costume jewellery and finally promises to give the little man her first-born child once she is queen.

Everything goes according to plan and the miller's daughter marries the king who, for tax reasons, has stopped asking her to produce gold. But when the first child is born, the gnome appears again and demands his dues. The queen offers him all her (now genuine) jewellery but the little man stubbornly insists on the child. Only when she turns on the waterworks does he relent and give her three days grace to find out his name. If she does she will be allowed to keep the child.

Now the queen sends out her messengers who drive around the country far and wide to find out the little man's name, but without success. Only on the third day does one messenger come back to report that he saw a little man dancing around a fire, singing in a falsetto voice and rather off-key, 'Little does my lady dream, Rumpelstiltskin in my name.'

Now the queen knows the gnome's name, and when he returns she tells him, whereupon he loses his temper and stamps his foot into the ground and in his rage pulls at his leg so fiercely that he tears himself in two. The queen has one of her servants come in and clear up the mess and lives happily ever after.

The sequel:

LET us assume that the whole story had taken place when the miller's daughter was 26 rather than 16. In the meantime, Pippa has passed her university degree in chemical engineering and is working for a pharmaceutical company in a nearby town. Her father is concerned about the fact that his daughter is single at her age and is therefore still going around, praising her beauty and intelligence, hoping to find a suitor who will take her off his hands.

As the royal deliverer of wholemeal breakfast rolls, he is invited to the king's annual garden party.

Progress: Professional diversification results in improved business connections.

He seizes this opportunity to put his case to the king. As he is awaiting his audience, he has a few glasses to steady his nerves and so enters the royal study not altogether sober. The king, whose finances are chronically low, listens attentively to the miller's slightly slurred speech and, in anticipation of a solution to his cash flow problems, orders Pippa to the palace the next day when he eagerly presents her with a room full of straw and a spinning wheel. A short argument ensues where Pippa insists that her professional experience has led her to the conclusion that it is impossible to turn straw into gold and that she cannot do anything without her Bunsen burner anyway, but the king suspects her of simply being work-shy and locks her into the room, threatening her with physical harm if she doesn't produce the gold by morning.

As Pippa sits on a bale of straw, wondering what on earth to do about her predicament, the door opens and a peculiar little man of unpleasant physical appearance enters the room. He politely introduces himself as Mister Rumpel Stiltskin.

Progress: **Good manners further business relations.**

He explains that he is a financial adviser who works at alchemy as a hobby in his spare time. He also reveals that after years of experimenting he has finally managed to develop a chemical formula which makes it possible to convert fodder plants into 18 carat gold, patent pending. He offers to demonstrate this process to the girl, free of charge, hoping that Pippa will be impressed by his skills and consequently fall in love with him.

Progress: **Generosity creates goodwill.**

(Rumpel has not had a lot of success with women so far because of his diminutive stature and the scar tissue on his face which is the result of a number of explosions during test runs in his laboratory.)

When the king appears the next morning, all the straw has gone and Pippa, to his delight, presents him with a gold bar of considerable size. In euphoric mood, the king orders her to stay around, and after conferring with his accountant, asks her to convert the straw in an even larger room into gold.

Again, Rumpel Stiltskin visits during the night, rapidly transforms the straw and spends the rest of the night chatting to Pippa. He knows he has not won her over yet, but as he has been on a stress management course, he no longer needs to rip himself in half when things don't go his way.

> *Progress:* **Working on your weak points and improving them leads to a healthier and longer life.**

He gets her attention by proposing a lucrative business deal to her, with himself running the production side and Pippa managing the marketing and distribution side of their gold manufacturing business. Pippa, who has always dreamed of going self-employed, agrees happily.

The next morning the king is presented with an even larger bar of gold and, delirious with joy and greed, begins to babble about marriage if Pippa can just do one more room of straw for him. Pippa, who has no intention of becoming the wife of the potbellied monarch, promises to do as she is told. When Rumpel lets himself into the room with his masterkey she tells him about the king's plans and the two decide to elope to a foreign country that night, but not before turning the last batch of straw into gold as consolation for the king.

> *Progress:* **A secure financial future makes generosity possible.**

Later on, Rumpel has cosmetic surgery and he and Pippa get married, and they live happily ever after.

SLEEPING BEAUTY

The story so far:

THE king and queen of a country are very upset because they have all the riches in the world but no children. They try for years and years, go from doctor to doctor, but nothing helps. Finally they give up all hope and decide to go on a holiday to Bermuda. When they get back they find to their great delight that the queen is expecting, and nine months later a healthy baby girl is born. At the christening, the royal couple invite all the fairies they can find in their kingdom so that every one of them can bestow a special gift on the little princess.

Suddenly the doors fly open and an eighth fairy sweeps in, fuming with rage because she has not been invited. The king and queen are very apologetic and try to appease the indignant fairy, but to little avail. She puts a spell on the princess, saying that she will prick her finger on a spindle and die. Luckily the seventh fairy has not bestowed her gift yet, but rather than saying that the grumpy fairy's spell should be null and void, she nervously decides that the princess will not die but fall into a deep sleep that will last a hundred years, at the end of which she shall be awakened by a king's son. The royal couple are beside themselves with grief and the king insists on having all spindles banned in the kingdom.

All goes well for sixteen years, but one evening when her parents are out to a charity function, the princess decides to explore the east wing of the castle and climbs up into the tower. There she finds a little old lady, spinning away with a spindle. The princess is of course fascinated by the spindle which is a new thing to her. When she tries to spin, however, she pricks her finger and falls into a deep sleep.

Her parents are devastated. The seventh fairy waves her magic wand over everyone and they all fall asleep.

A hundred years on, a foreign king's son goes hunting and notices the castle amid a thick wood of trees. His friends try to put him off by telling him the castle is haunted, but an old man assures him that a beautiful princess is sleeping in there, so the prince decides to do what a man's got to do. He gets his men to clear a way through the brambles so as not to ruin his designer clothes and then he finds himself in front of the castle door which is ajar. He enters and begins to search the castle for the princess. As there are numerous wings and even more numerous rooms it takes him quite a while, but finally, after another two weeks, he finds the princess. He kisses her and she wakes up and demands breakfast. As the prince is not used to doing any household chores, he has to go and kiss all the kitchen maids, and the princess gets really mad at him, but later they make up and live happily ever after.

The sequel:

So WHAT would have happened if Princess Zoe had escaped the curse of the eighth fairy for another ten years? No doubt she would have grown into a pretty thing with lots of admirers who block the gravelled driveway to the castle by day and by night with their sportscars. By now the gossip columnists are busy speculating which of the young men is going to be the lucky one, and the betting shop business flourishes. However, Zoe has no intention of getting married just yet, preferring to go around the local antique shops to see if she can pick up some bargains.

The old lady in the tower of the east wing has by now been pensioned off and lives in an old people's home by the seaside. Everyone is happy and the peculiar incident at the christening has been all but forgotten.

One day when Princess Zoe is rummaging around in a box in a second hand shop she comes across an old spindle which she decides to buy without really knowing what it is. When she takes it home, her mother is horrified because she suddenly remembers the curse. The queen becomes very agitated and tries to take the spindle away from Zoe who won't let go of it, and in the struggle, the queen pricks herself on the spindle. As soon as Zoe sees the drop of blood oozing out of her mother's finger, she passes out and collapses into the arms of her bodyguard. The queen is inconsolable, the king desolate. They try the kiss of life, cold water, scents and her favourite pop record, but Zoe remains unconscious. The royal physician diagnoses shock and recommends strict bed rest for the princess.

Ten years go by and Zoe is still in a coma, only kept alive by being fed her favourite dishes like beef stroganoff and spaghetti bolognaise intravenously. People around her go into new jobs, retire or die, but Zoe remains the same.

Fifty years later, everyone in the palace has passed away, including the gardeners, and the grounds of the castle begin to delapidate rapidly, with bushes and brambles getting out of control and forming a veritable wall around the castle.

When a foreign prince passes through the area he is interested in visiting the castle which is marked as a listed building in his tourist guide. When he finds the driveway, overgrown by shrubs, he gets his electric hedge trimmer out of the back of his Landrover and sets to work. In less than a day he has managed to cut through the thicket and is able to drive up to the castle.

>**Progress: Modern technology is a valuable tool.**
>**After all, time is money!**

With the help of his tourist guide he locates the princess's bedroom immediately and is just in time to kiss Zoe awake before the last bottle on the drip runs out. When Zoe opens her eyes she is faced with the handsome foreigner who, thanks to proper schooling, is able to converse fluently with the princess in her own language.

>**Progress: Knowledge of foreign languages enhances and furthers communication between nations.**

It is love at first sight. They get married and turn the castle into a five-star hotel which earns them enough money never to have to work again in their life, which is what they were accustomed to anyway, and they live happily ever after.

HANSEL AND GRETEL

The story so far:

I TAKE this opportunity to put right a story which is to be found in children's books in a badly contorted version. You may have heard a story where two children are abandoned in the woods by their parents because they are so poor that they cannot feed them any more. After an initially unsuccessful attempt to get rid of the children the plot succeeds and the children fail to find their way back home. Instead they wander around in the forest for a few days, until they finally arrive at the gingerbread house of a wicked witch and start to eat bits off the house because they are so desperately hungry. The witch pretends to be helpful and kind and lulls the children into a false sense of security, only to tell them later that she has every intention of eating Hansel once he is fat enough. She locks him in a cage and checks whether he has grown any fatter by feeling his finger, but the clever little boy, realising she is shortsighted, holds out a bone. After a while the witch is fed up with waiting and decides to eat him anyway, but Gretel manages to push the old witch into the oven and kill her. The children then return home, guided by the animals of the forest. The precious stones and pearls they have taken from the witch's house help them and their parents to live in comfort henceforth.

What really happened:

HANSEL and Gretel are a couple of teenagers who have managed to cause their mother two nervous breakdowns and driven their father to drink. They are obnoxious middle-class brats who play truant from school, steal and dabble in drugs. One day Hansel and Gretel decide to go for a daytrip on their motorbikes without telling their parents, who are somewhat relieved at the sudden disappearance of their offspring. Much to their disappointment the youngsters are returned a day later by the police who have caught them stealing from a supermarket.

By systematically forbidding them to leave the house, the parents manage to entice Hansel and Gretel to run away again, this time to a forest in the countryside, where the youngsters proceed to frighten animals and ramblers alike by turning up the volume on their radio-cassette full blast. Just as they are beginning to get really hungry they come across a little white house, beautifully kept and surrounded by a garden full of organically grown vegetables and flowers. They go up to the front door and shout and bang until a little old lady with a hearing aid appears, asking them politely what they want. Hansel and Gretel demand a meal of hamburgers and chips with tomato ketchup and a bottle of beer each because they are hungry and thirsty. As they have a foot in the door already, the old lady has to let them in, and the teenagers stomp into the living room without bothering to wipe their muddy boots, leaving dirt tracks all over the well-polished parquet floor. They help themselves from the fruit bowl without asking, put their feet up on the table and use the table cloth to wipe their noses while the old lady hurries to supply them with a cooked meal. She watches in horror as the youngsters slouch over their plates, both elbows on the table, noisily slurping their soup and speaking with their mouths full. When they have finished their meal, Hansel burps loudly to distract the old lady's attention while Gretel pinches the piggy bank from the sideboard and pockets the pension book and a handful of jewellery from one of the drawers. They leave without saying thank you and bang the door on the way out. When they get home they find that their parents have moved without leaving a forwarding address.

The sequel:

LET us transport the entire story forward in time. Hansel and Gretel are now in their twenties and are still the same good-for-nothings that they were ten years ago. Because of their frequent absences from school they didn't get any qualifications and had to get jobs as property developers (property developers please note: this is only a fairy tale!). They were forced into the humiliating situation of seeking work because their parents refused point blank to leave their holiday home on the Costa del Sol to come home and support their offspring financially.

Progress: Financial problems further personal development.

However, to their great relief, Hansel and Gretel find that they can earn a lot of money with a minimum of effort, so one Wednesday they decide to close the office for the day and go for a drive in the countryside instead, trying out their brand new BMW company car. As they buzz along the road, they come across a beautiful little house in a wooded area. Spontaneously they decide to drop in on the owner and see if they can manipulate him into selling the property cheaply so that they can sell it at a much inflated price and make a huge profit on it later. In order to preserve the value of a potential future asset to their business, they decide to ring the bell rather than kick the door in as they did so many years ago.

Progress: **Good manners further business relations.**

After a moment the door is opened by a little old lady who immediately recognises her visitors as the obnoxious couple of kids who ruined her place all those years ago. She asks them in and, upon their polite request, shows them around the house. As Hansel and Gretel inspect the rooms they pass depreciatory remarks about the state of the house to pave the way for a low price offer. They pretend to find fault with the carpets, the walls, the kitchen units and the window frames, pointing out to each other how the ceiling in the dining room needs painting and the walls redecorating. The old lady listens to all of this for a long time without comment, but finally she agrees that the dining room would look a lot better with a fresh coat of paint on the ceilings and new wallpaper on the walls.

She asks her visitors to take a seat while she fetches something for them. Hansel and Gretel gloat in anticipatory triumph, convinced that the deal is in the bag. When the old lady returns she carries in rolls and rolls of wallpaper and several pots of white paint, apple blossom shade, matt. She sets the lot down in front of Hansel and Gretel and tells them she reckons they owe her a favour.

Progress: **Making demands on others puts a stop to exploitation.**

She reminds them of their unruly behaviour when she, very kindly, supplied them with a three-course meal all those years ago and points out that splashes of tomato ketchup can still be found on the walls of the dining room where they had their meal. She stresses that it would only be fair for them to make up for it now and redecorate those walls as she is too old to attempt this job herself. Hansel and Gretel are first of all speechless at this proposition and then break out into hearty laughter. No way are they going to do this!

The little old lady leaves the room without a word and returns with her two pet Rottweiler dogs who are the size of young cows but a lot less friendly looking. As they approach Hansel and Gretel, the dogs start growling unpleasantly and only stop when the two reach for the paintbrushes. As Hansel and Gretel scrape old paper off and put new paper onto the walls and paint the new paper, the dogs don't let them out of their sight, just growling occasionally when the two involuntary labourers dare pause for a moment. Meanwhile, the old lady goes for a spin in Hansel and Gretel's BMW, enjoying the fine weather and beautiful landscape around her.

Progress: Pets provide you with hours of pleasure. Everyone should have one!

When she returns, the dining room is finished and so are Hansel and Gretel. She thanks them politely for their help and sends them on their way.

The next day she rings her local estate agent to put her newly decorated house on the market.

PART II

MANY people are dissatisfied with their present situation in life. They are bored or frustrated with their job, feel they are being over- or underworked or that there is no opportunity to use their full potential in their current position. Others are unhappy about the relationship they are in and would like to get out; others again are discontented about still living with their parents. So why don't all these people do something about the situation they are so unhappy about? Surely there is nothing easier than picking up a paper and looking for a new job! Or packing your bags and moving out! And yet these people will dilly-dally and remain where they are, sometimes for years, before they make a move, waiting and hoping that things and people around them will change so that they are relieved of the burden of having to make a decision themselves. This is a bit like the drunk man who stands on the pavement holding out his doorkey in front of him, and when asked what he is doing replies, 'I have heard that the earth is turning. I'm waiting for my house to come by.'

Taking action to implement changes in one's life can seem to be very hazardous. There is always the possibility that you will make the wrong choice or that the new situation will be even worse than the old one. If only someone were there to wave a magic wand. . . Remaining as you are seems so much safer in view of all the uncertainties that appear to lurk behind the new options, and no excuse is too feeble to postpone making that change or taking that decision.

Let us look at some of these excuses and examine them for validity.

6. THE MYTH OF 'THE RIGHT TIME'

BARBARA was head over heels in love with Graham. She adored him because he was gentle, understanding and great fun to be with, and there was nothing she would have liked better than to spend more time with him. Unfortunately she couldn't because she was still married to John. Her marriage had been on the rocks for many years now. They had been childhood sweethearts and got married very young because Barbara was expecting a baby. A second child followed a few years later, but the marriage soon turned stale. They grew apart and felt they had nothing to say to each other, each living in their own lonely world, kept together only by their teenage children. And along came Graham, a divorcee who worked in the same profession as Barbara. They felt close to each other from the start, talking easily and feeling in harmony with one another. Graham asked Barbara to come and live with him and she promised to do so, but not just yet because her son was taking A-levels and she didn't want to upset him. Graham understood this and waited patiently; after all, the exams were only six months away.

When Barbara's son had passed his exams, Graham brought up the subject again, asking Barbara to tell her husband that she was going to leave him. But Barbara felt she couldn't do so just then because John was in the process of going abroad for work for a couple of months; she promised to speak to him once he was back. But when he came back she couldn't tell him because she didn't want to spoil his return for him, and anyway, she felt that her 15-year-old daughter was too young to deal with a separation. Graham assured her that he was happy to have her daughter stay with them, but Barbara didn't like the idea.

Graham waited for four years and then decided to accept an offer for a job abroad. He had given up hope that Barbara would ever take the step and leave her marriage. Barbara was deeply unhappy and upset that Graham had decided to go when it was only another two years until her daughter left school, and then she would definitely leave John – unless of course he was in a difficult work situation at the time. Half a year later, John left Barbara for another woman.

Barbara had been waiting for the 'right time', the right moment to break the news to John and the children. She didn't want to do it while any member of her family was in a weak or vulnerable position. Neither did she want to do it when the family was happy, for example on John's return from his assignment. Barbara did not want to take the responsibility for causing her family's unhappiness because then she could not have enjoyed being with Graham. Had she been honest with herself she would have had to admit that it was simply too daunting a prospect to face John with her decision to leave him. She had been afraid to face his hurt and his anger. And she had also been afraid of what the future might hold and how she would cope without her children.

Very often the excuse of having to wait for the right time masks a fear of taking a step in a new direction, even though this step may promise a happier life in the long run.

There is no denying that it takes courage to leave your old surroundings, and sometimes only extreme external pressure can push a person into making that change. And even then there is no guarantee that the new situation is going to be more satisfactory than the old one; but then life is not about guarantees, it is about opportunities. Apart from complicating matters, procrastination just prolongs your own unhappiness, and the longer you allow an unpleasant situation to continue, the harder it is to amend it later.

Janet, a young mother of two, felt very resentful towards her husband because he left her several evenings a week to go to his fitness club. As his profession took him away from home frequently, Janet felt that she had to shoulder the burden of household and children all by herself, and she wanted her husband to give her some support. Besides, Janet would have liked to go out herself but didn't feel she should leave the children with a babysitter. She was unhappy because her husband wasn't 'pulling his weight', as she put it, when it came to sharing responsibility for the children. Janet had been very active before she had the children, travelling a lot and seeing her friends frequently. Now she felt socially isolated and very discontented about it. She felt her husband was having all the good times, while she was stuck at home with the children day in, day out.

To start off with, she had accepted her husband's frequent absences. She didn't want to nag and, after all, she loved him and he was working so hard all week. . . She was hoping that, as time went by, she would get used to the situation, but this never happened. After three years, Janet had started to become impatient with her children and felt hostile towards her husband, even though she tried very hard to be tolerant and to suppress her feelings of anger. Although she occasionally mentioned her discontent to her husband, she never took any active steps to get an evening off for herself. Maybe when the children were bigger. . . In the meantime she was getting more and more restless and moody and her relationship with her husband had started to deteriorate.

When Janet came to see me she expressed great anger at her husband for his frequent absences in his spare time. On examining her situation more closely, however, it turned out that her main concern was the fact that she felt she would be a bad mother if she left her children with a babysitter rather than look after them herself. Also, she thought she needed to be home when her husband arrived back from work in the evening.

First of all we established that her own unhappiness was making her family just as unhappy as herself and that it was her duty to see to her own happiness in order to be a good mother and wife. She was not doing anyone a favour by remaining discontented, so it was up to her to become more contented, and one way of achieving that was to create some time for herself, away from home.

Her first step was to speak to her husband about her plan. To her surprise, he proved to be cooperative and agreed to look after the children for one evening a week. Also, he saw no problem in getting a babysitter to stay in with the children should he be away himself. On this occasion, the couple had a heart-to-heart talk and also decided to spend more time together as a family. Janet went on to ensure she had time to herself once a week and see friends on that evening and reported that she felt a lot better for it. She became more relaxed and optimistic again and the only question that remained for her was why she hadn't made that change three years ago.

What would have happened had she waited for 'the right time'? Would she eventually have got used to being tied to home and children? I doubt it very much, judging from the state Janet was in when she came to see me.

What time would have been 'the right time' anyway? When the children started school? When they were over 10? How do you define 'the right time'? However many reasons you find that speak *for* a particular point in time, you can easily find as many reasons that speak *against* it; in other words, you will still have to make a decision.

A right time as such does not really exist, so it is pointless waiting for it to come. What does exist is your own feelings, and if they are negative and you are beginning to feel unhappy then that is your signal that the time has come to do something about it.

7. THE MYTH OF 'SECURITY'

PEOPLE often oppose change because they are afraid of what might await them in the future. No matter how drab the job, no matter how unsatisfactory the partner, it still appears safer to stay put than to venture out into new fields, even if the new option promises to be more rewarding than the present state of affairs. The proverbial devil you know has a greater hold over us than we care to admit.

Frequently the reluctance to leave a boring job is hidden behind the excuse that one wants to 'stick it out', waiting for circumstances to change, hoping that one day the boss recognises your worth and offers you a promotion. But somehow, this never happens. So you stay with the company for another year, or maybe two, still waiting and hoping – and still nothing happens.

Bob had gone through just that. He acted as assistant manager in the office services department of a large organisation and had been running the department for two years because the office manager was off sick very often. Bob had three people working under him and proved an efficient organiser and competent manager. He was well liked by everyone and had displayed outstanding leadership qualities over the three years he had been with the company. He was not very happy with his salary though, as it failed to reflect the responsibilities the job carried. Even when he took over his boss's job during her long absences, he was kept in the lower wage band, without even as much as paid overtime. Still, Bob decided to remain with the company because it was, after all, a secure job. He also wanted to wait and see what would happen once his superior was pensioned off in eight months time. Everyone was sure that he would be offered the post.

When the time came he was not even invited for an interview for the vacancy. Instead, the company recruited someone from outside who was presented to the department as the new boss one Monday morning. In a departmental reshuffle, Bob was demoted from assistant manager to ordinary staff member. He finally decided to leave the company, angry and disappointed at having wasted valuable years which could have been spent elsewhere to further his career.

Shirley had started her new job with great enthusiasm. The job description promised varied and interesting work and Shirley soon found herself happily involved in learning everything there was to learn, enjoying the challenge of her new position. After a year her boss left and was replaced by a new manager who decided to fundamentally restructure the department. Amongst other things he decided to take away quite a few areas that Shirley had been running all by herself, leaving her with secretarial tasks such as typing, filing and making his appointments. Shirley was very upset and felt she had been demoted, even though her salary stayed the same. She finally picked up courage to speak to her boss about the situation, but he just brushed her complaints aside. Shirley felt discouraged and humiliated by her boss's brusque dismissal of her objections. She felt that she was not appreciated and that the effort and commitment she had displayed in the past had been ignored. She complained bitterly to all her friends and colleagues and felt thoroughly miserable with her lot. She had given up hoping for any positive changes but did not feel she wanted to look for another job. After all, she knew her present job inside out, even though it was boring. At the end of three years, the department was closed down and Shirley and her boss were made redundant.

An unsatisfactory job situation can lead to great upset; people get impatient and angry when they feel that their talents go unnoticed and that their commitment is not rewarded. They may even mention their discontent to their boss who promises to look into the matter, but often nothing happens for months on end. People will then feel reluctant to bring up the subject again because they are afraid of being marked down as trouble-makers. Many an ulcer and nervous breakdown is due to repressed anger and frustration and could be avoided if people could find the courage to address the topic again with their boss or to look for alternative employment. Although they are fed up with their job, they don't want to leave the security they think it gives them, not realising that this security is illusory.

The price you pay for remaining in a distressing situation without doing anything about it is high. It can cost you your health and, in extreme cases, your life. If stress builds up over a long period of time without being released, your physical or emotional health can break down.

It is irrelevant whether this happens in a professional or a private setting. As long as you use the excuse of security to avoid having to make changes, you are digging your own emotional grave. Being discontented not only has effects on your health, it also undermines your family life because you are bound to bring your irritation home. The higher your discontent with your work situation the higher your risk of splitting up with your partner.

Thinking that we are secure only if we do not move means that we are deceiving ourselves. We can always be dismissed by our employer or left by our partner, through no fault of our own. We can always be demoted, the company can always close down, and all of this is beyond our control. Refusing to express our wishes because we are afraid of rocking the boat and jeopardising our 'safe' job or our 'safe' relationship can result in us getting landed with things we don't want to do, and although the job or the relationship is still safe for the time being, our health and well-being is not. It is everyone's personal choice whether they want to be chronically unhappy or whether they want to take the plunge into a new venture and create more favourable circumstances for themselves.

8. THE MYTH OF 'MODESTY'

THE issue of modesty is one that seems particularly prominent in women. Very often, it is considered wrong for a woman to aspire to a better job, a better education or a better financial position. Even today, girls are brought up to be pleasant and accommodating, making others feel comfortable and important in the hope of being liked or loved in return. They are taught to be unassuming and unpretentious and stay out of the limelight.

This self-effacing attitude can be a great stumbling block on the way up the career ladder. If you feel that everyone else is better and more deserving than you are, it is very unlikely that you will go for that higher position, simply because you feel awkward about publicly admitting that you feel competent to tackle it.

Irene had been working as a personal assistant to a lecturer at a business college when she heard that a vacancy was coming up for a registrar of one of the courses. Even though Irene felt confident that she could cope with the post, and although she was keen on a change, she felt unable to apply because she worried about what would happen if she didn't get the job: it would be too much like being reproached for not knowing her place. She was convinced that if she went for the interview and 'admitted' that she thought she was capable of mastering the job, her immodesty would be punished. She therefore decided not to apply and found that the job was given to a girl who she considered to be far less competent than herself.

Another problem that arises through a false sense of modesty is that of salary increases. Many companies will assess their employees once a year, and often this includes a self-assessment as part of the procedure. Woman often find it difficult to point out their achievements and draw their boss's attention to the fact that they work efficiently and that they have performed well during the year. Women are generally more reticent than men in asking their boss for a rise.

Caroline had been working for a tour operator for several years. She had never been particularly pleased with her salary and although she had, very feebly, addressed the topic with her boss, she was never given the increase she felt she should have. Recently she had become really upset when she found that a new employee was on a higher salary than she, even though the new colleague held a lower position. Caroline felt frustrated and angry at this injustice but told her friends that she was not able to point out all her achievements to her boss. She would rather stay on the lower salary and look for a job elsewhere. This is, of course, a losing strategy, because a similar situation may well arise with the new employer and then she would be faced with the same problem again.

If you want to achieve something professionally, it is important to learn to blow your own trumpet. This is not the same thing as showing off or putting yourself above others; it is standing up to be counted. Everyone has his or her own strong points, and you need to be aware of them when you want to advance in your job. This doesn't mean that you should sweep your shortcomings under the carpet, on the contrary. It is equally important to look at your weaknesses and to work on them, but when you are going for a promotion or a rise you need to have your positive points at your fingertips because if you don't believe in yourself it is unlikely that the personnel manager or your potential new boss is going to believe in you.

Publicising your own achievements in an effective and non-aggressive way is a skill that can be learned. Just because you have been hiding your light under a bushel for the last twenty years does not mean that you have to do so for the rest of your life. If you have the desire to progress in your job you should not let yourself be hampered by old-fashioned views. Look at the people who praise modesty as a virtue: they are without exception either people who have never achieved anything themselves, or people who are worried that your advancement may get in the way of their own.

There is nothing wrong with acknowledging that you are doing your job well and that you are successful. Part of being successful is to know your own worth and to communicate it.

It is interesting to see how difficult it seems to be for people to talk about their good points. In my stress management workshops, I usually hand out sheets entitled 'What I like about myself'. People take a long time to come up with the required three points, whereas the sheet 'My shortcomings' is very quickly filled to the bottom of the page. Maybe we are more aware of our faults because they were continually pointed out to us in childhood, but we can certainly learn to be more positive about ourselves and to emphasise our successes rather than our failures.

Overcoming a debilitating sense of modesty is also impor-tant because it helps us deal with criticism more construc-tively. Nobody likes to have their faults or shortcomings pointed out to them, but there are vast differences between the ways people deal with criticism. The scale extends from ignoring other people's faultfinding to being totally shattered by it, depending on how well-developed your self-esteem is. Thinking that you cannot possibly ever be wrong and there-fore ignoring criticism certainly displays an unhealthy lack of self-knowledge and modesty, just as accepting all criticism unquestioningly is a sign of exaggerated meekness. It is essen-tial for you to be aware of your own strengths and good points because they form the basis of your self-esteem, and the more solidly this basis is built the better it is going to hold out when you are being criticised.

When someone objects to what we are saying or doing, it usually means that our actions make them feel uncomfortable or anxious for some reason. It does not mean, however, that we are worthless because we aroused someone else's objec-tions. As long as our self-esteem is still intact we can calmly listen to criticism and deal with it by negotiating or arguing our own point with the other person, and finally reaching a solution or compromise. We may even end up having to reject the other person's objections, but this is an entirely different kettle of fish from rejecting criticism outright.

Constructively dealing with criticism implies listening carefully to another's point of view and ensuring that you understand what the *real* problem is. As we have seen in Janet's case (see p. 33), her official complaint was with her husband, whereas the real reason for her unhappiness was her struggle with her new role as a mother.

Working on building up your self-confidence and ensuring that you are doing at least some of the things that are important to you enable you to cope with verbal battles a lot better, and as we cannot expect to go through life without ever being criticised, this is a valuable ability to have.

9. The myth of 'dependency'

ANOTHER excuse which is frequently made to avoid having to make changes in one's life is that of not being a free agent. 'I cannot do anything without my husband, and we are just not interested in the same things, so I won't go to evening classes' or 'My mother doesn't approve of me going out at weekends, so I cannot really have a fulfilled social life.' In other words, you make out that you want to expand your horizons, that you want to progress and move into new areas of interest, but you cannot do so because others fail to give you support or because others disapprove of your plans; and because these other people are close relatives or friends you feel you have to live your life according to their rules or their advice and that there is nothing you can do about your dependency on their opinion.

The fact is, though, that the only person who really knows what is good for you is you. If you feel the need to see your friends more often, to take up a hobby or to progress in your job, then that is what is best for you. If you are old enough to go out and buy this book yourself, you are old enough to know what is best for you. When others assure you that they only want what is best for you, what they really mean is that they want what is best for them, and these could be two entirely different things. A son who feels restricted at home may decide that he wants to spend more time away from home, going out with friends. His mother, however, may call him selfish and tell him that his place is at home by her side on the grounds that she does not have anyone else and would be lonely if he went out every weekend.

This is of course a difficult argument to object to because the son does not want his mother to be lonely nor does he want to be considered selfish, and in cases like this you can easily give up your own interests in order to remain in the other person's good books. But the mother's request for the son's company every weekend is just as selfish as it would be if the son went out every single weekend. If the son gives in to the mother's demand and stays at home he is bound to resent this emotional blackmail and will not make good company for his mother.

For this reason it is very important for both sides to find an acceptable compromise where everyone gets some of what they need. It is not a solution to abandon the mother altogether, but neither is it a solution for the son to stay with her all the time. Both of them are responsible for their own welfare, and each of them has to work on finding entertainment for themselves which does not involve the other person. Only then will the relationship remain on pleasant terms.

If you feel that you are unable to do a new thing without your partner by your side, then you are giving in to an illusion. Many widowed and divorced people discover that they can cope on their own when they really have to. But as long as the other person is around, the feeling of dependency and insecurity outweighs the promises of an interesting new venture. But isn't it so much safer and easier to start new things when you have a supportive partner in the background? The mother who finds it so difficult to let her son go and lead his own life is really afraid of doing just that, namely to go and make a life for herself. As long as the son is around she doesn't have to face this task.

It is easy to get into a habit pattern of always relying on another person to be there and to give up striving for your own personal goals. Within a family, a father can easily forget that he is more than a husband and wage-earner; a mother can easily forget that she is more than a housewife and nanny; and children can be made to forget that they have their own individual talents and inclinations. Even though all members have to compromise in order to make the family work, they also need to follow their individual dreams and aims in order to feel happy and fulfilled.

There is only so much we can blame on others. The time comes where we have to take responsibility for ourselves and attempt to make some of our dreams come true, or we will end up looking back over our life and discovering that we were a dutiful father or mother, son or daughter, husband or wife, but that we have not lived our own life and achieved our own personal goals.

The midlife-crisis is such a point in time. You look back and realise that you have not done what you set out to do, that you are still looking for an achievement which will give you deep satisfaction – and time is running out! But a crisis can only arise when you think that it is too late to change. Breaking out of marriage or having an affair may be a temporary relief from that crisis but it does not solve the underlying problem. True independence is inner independence. No other person can give you independence. As soon as you involve another person you create a certain amount of dependence, whether you want to or not. Independence means standing on your own two feet, making your own decisions and accepting responsibility for them.

Personal development can be achieved under the most unlikely circumstances. All you need to have is a goal and to keep it firmly in your mind. Personal development is not dependent on other people's help or approval, on relevant schooling or your financial situation; it is only dependent on your determination to change things for the better. You are as dependent or independent as you want to be.

10. PROBLEMS ARE PRESENTS

HAVING a problem means that things are not going according to plan. When we cannot find a pair of grey shoes to buy we have a problem because now we cannot wear that grey outfit to the party. When the boss is unreasonable we have a problem because we are getting upset about it. When the girlfriend only wants to go to expensive restaurants and we are constantly broke we have a problem because we either have a disgruntled girlfriend on our hands or an overdrawn bank account.

A situation is problematic when it disrupts the smooth running of events as we projected them. We perceive things as going 'wrong' when we cannot have exactly what we want at exactly the time we want it, and immediately these hiccups jeopardise the entire enterprise. Or at least we behave as if that were the case. We get angry, frustrated, dejected or irritable when life does not oblige with the prompt and straightforward fulfilment of our wishes. But is this really the only way to react to problems? It certainly isn't the best!

Problems are useful in many respects and not as disruptive as we commonly think. What causes us to panic is our imagination that suddenly starts working overtime. When we encounter an obstacle we tend to go into despair-mode, behaving as if our entire venture will fail; we worry and fret and are ready to give up. It is strange to think that we have met obstacles hundreds of times and have in most cases overcome them and yet we cannot stop getting upset when the next problem presents itself.

As a rule, life does not run smoothly. It doesn't for the losers in life, but it doesn't for the winners either. The only difference between these two categories is that the losers give up while the winners persist. When you read about famous people in magazines and newspapers, it all sounds so easy and straightforward, as if these people had just sailed to the top unhindered and unhampered, ingeniously choosing all the best options and unerringly making for their destination. But it doesn't work like that; the papers are only giving us the synopsis. When you sum up someone's career, you pick out the main points and make them into a string of events which appear to lead directly to the goal. We rarely hear about the complications these people met on their way to success, the difficulties they had to overcome and the obstructions they had to conquer. And even when you have reached the peak of success you are not safe from the bumps in the road of life, but at least you are in the financial position to afford better shock absorbers.

Since we cannot but acknowledge the existence of disruptive events intruding into our plans, we may as well make the best of them. They are part and parcel of everyday life and should be accepted as such. The less you resist them the calmer you will stay and the better you will be able to deal with them.

It is like travelling on a road to your dream-castle and constantly coming across barricades across the road. You can either get really upset and pummel the obstacle with your little fists, or you can look carefully at the obstacle and think of how you can overcome it. Is it made of wood or brick? Is there a gap somewhere that allows you to slip through without having to dismantle it? Can you climb it or walk round it or shift it? If you can't think of an answer, is there someone who can? Spend time thinking about a solution so as to expend as little emotional energy as possible on the problem, preserving your energy to pursue your ultimate aim.

Problems need to be faced in order to be solved, but don't allocate greater importance to them than they deserve. Keep your sight firmly focused on your final destination and you will get there, no matter how many obstacles you have to climb, knock down, push over or walk around.

Once we have learned to deal with problems constructively they turn out to have a positive effect on us. The ups and downs of life keep us flexible and help us to develop new skills, make us adopt different perspectives and give us a greater feeling of control over our life. If we look at problems as a challenge rather than a threat we can use them to our advantage and they can become important stepping stones on our way to a fulfilled and happy life.

11. THE PETER PAN SYNDROME

J. M. BARRIE called his play 'Peter Pan, or The Boy Who Wouldn't Grow Up'. The hero is an invincible boy with magic powers who takes the children Wendy, John and Michael into Never-Never-Land where adults cannot go. The storyline is a mixture of dream and nightmare: the children have to brave adverse situations, fight pirates and pass a variety of tests, but in spite of fierce battles, no blood is shed, good triumphs over bad and every adventure comes to a happy end. Never-Never-Land is a world far from reality, a world where there is no need for children to obey their parents, and for Peter Pan, Never-Never-Land constitutes the only reality there is. He doesn't acknowledge anything outside his kingdom and denies that real life outside is a big adventure. This is why, in the end, he rejects the offer from Wendy's mother to come and live with them.

Depending on the sort of childhood you have had, you will have formed an image of what it means to be an adult. If you were raised in an environment where adults were sensible people who enjoyed life and appeared to be in control of events, growing up becomes something to look forward to. If, however, the adults around you seemed depressed and without enthusiasm, or always in a bad mood, the prospect of growing up can be rather daunting. The fact that children have only limited knowledge of what possibilities there are in life restricts their view of the world, and as long as their view is thus limited, they are unable to see what options life has to offer and how to make the best of them. They live in their own little world where the unknown and the unexplained are frightening and have mystical qualities which are beyond their control. It is only when difficulties and new situations are faced and worked through that the child learns to integrate them as additional knowledge to his world; this consequently helps widen his horizon. When, however, people get over-loaded with traumatic situations, we can observe the reverse movement, namely a withdrawal from the outside world and a retracting of the boundaries, and this can result in the inability to leave the house (agoraphobia) or in the unwilling-ness to communicate or interact with others (depression).

The Peter Pan syndrome consists of various attitudes that prevent people from becoming part of the adult world or advancing in their personal development beyond a certain stage once they are adults. Some of these attitudes are out-lined and discussed below.

FEAR OF EXPLORING REALITY OUTSIDE YOUR OWN

In this context, the expression 'reality' is used in an individ-ual sense. Each one of us constructs our own reality, builds our own mental image of how the world works and of what makes other people tick, so that every image is unique. By communicating with others we learn about their realities and we discover where our images overlap and where they differ. If we see the world in a similar way to someone, we are more likely to become friends than if our views differ widely. Finding another person who shares our attitudes is comforting and reassuring because it validates our own point of view and therefore gives us a feeling of strength and self-esteem. The more people agree with us, the better we feel about ourselves, the surer we are that we are right. Consequently, anything outside our own reality becomes an unwelcome intrusion and is regarded with suspicion. The club of bulldog-owners won't admit anyone who owns a Yorkshire terrier; the lesbian encounter group won't let men take part; the racist will not go out and get to know black people. The more time you spend in your club of same-thinkers, the less likely you are to expand your hor-izons, and the more likely you are to be upset by situations outside your own reality. As a rule of thumb one could say that the more fanatical people are about their views, the more they are afraid of realities outside their own.

This is not to say that it is wrong or harmful to share one's opinions with a lot of other people, on the contrary; we all need to feel accepted and supported by others. The point is that it is important to venture outside our own context every once in a while, or we will get stuck in a rut, become inflexible and age before our time.

FEAR OF TAKING RESPONSIBILITY FOR YOUR ACTIONS

We all have to make choices in our lives. These can be day-to-day decisions of what to do on a particular weekend or whether to buy a new dress, or they can be more far-reaching choices such as whether to commit ourselves financially in buying a new car, or whether we want children or not, or what profession we should choose to go into. As young children, we are relieved of making these decisions by our parents who will choose for us what we are going to wear today, which new school we are going to attend and what present we are taking to our friend's birthday party. Even though we may not like the choices that are made for us, we are still safe in the knowledge that, if anything goes wrong, we cannot be blamed for it because we didn't make the decision ourselves.

Some people never give up this attitude of blaming someone else, which is a sign that they got stuck in their development at an early stage. It is an unpleasant experience to be blamed for a mistake or a blunder, and the smaller your self-esteem the more likely you are to deny the error or to look for a scapegoat elsewhere, rather than owning up and taking responsibility for the wrong move you made. A family atmosphere where the child is harshly criticised for everything it does wrong without being given an opportunity to explain its position and its reasons can result in a fear of accepting responsibility later on in life, simply because by then the idea has been firmly instilled that if anything goes wrong there are unpleasnt consequences for you.

The fact remains, however, that sometime we will have to take over from our parents and make our own decisions and, above all, take responsibility for our own actions. If we decide to see some friends for a drink in a pub and then have an accident on the way back after drinking too much, we have acted in an irresponsible way and we need to acknowledge that fact and learn from it. One way of justifying yourself is saying that everyone else was drinking and you didn't want to be antisocial, and later when you realised you had had a few too many, you couldn't be bothered to use public transport or ask someone for a lift home. All these excuses are nothing but a denial that you had a *choice*. You had a choice to drink one pint rather than five, but your friends *made* you drink more than you wanted to. You had a choice of using public transport or of asking someone for a lift, but by that stage you had drunk enough not to care any more, so the *alcohol* made you irresponsible; you are innocent as driven snow. And this is how the list continues: we cannot get a better job because our parents didn't give us the right education; we cannot sleep at night because our boss overloads us with work during the day; we cannot be happy because we are overweight. Somewhere deep down inside we know that we should be doing something about these unsatisfactory situations, but somehow we never get around to it. This doesn't let us off the hook, though, because we are also responsible for the things we omit to do. Saying 'I *should* lose weight/get a new job/go on an assertiveness course' instead of 'If I really wanted to I *could* lose weight/get a new job/go on an assertiveness course' is refusing to make a positive decision, and that in itself is a decision. Not making a decision is also a decision. You are liable for the consequences of your decisions, be they active or passive ones.

If you don't run your life yourself, someone else is going to run it for you, and you may have to take what you get, rather than get what you want.

FEAR OF SAYING 'NO'

Compromise is a vital ingredient in a social environment because it makes it possible for a great number of people to live together and interact in a constructive way. Just as we cannot have a society where each individual does exactly as he or she pleases, we cannot have a society

where everyone is equal. Laws, rules and conventions are
attempts at bringing general issues to a rough common
denominator, but room has to be allowed for special circumstances. If you murder your father you are committing a
crime according to the law, but if it turns out that your
father has been abusing you for years the sentence may
well be modified or you are set free.

Compromising means negotiating so that you get at least
part of what you want. Problems arise when we compromise in situations that are unacceptable to us, when the
term 'compromise' becomes a euphemism for being unable
to say no. When you are in love with a girl who strings
you along and will not give up her other boyfriends, you
can compromise by saying that you are having a good time
with her anyway. This is fine as long as it doesn't bother
you that she is seeing other men. If it *does* bother you,
compromising is unacceptable because it is bad for your
self-esteem. A decision needs to be made which takes into
consideration your needs, and this decision may well be
that you end the relationship.

If you find it impossible to say no, you are not taking
yourself or your own needs very seriously. Other people
will notice that and treat you accordingly. Again, this attitude of self-negation is one of arrested development, a
residue of childhood. Initially, a child's world consists of
only the closest family, that is the parents and sisters and
brothers. They are all the child has in the world, and he
needs to be accepted and loved by the other members in
order to become a person. This child will do anything to
get this love, even deny his own feelings of anger or hate
if that love is not forthcoming. He cannot really afford those
negative feelings because if he shows them, the parents
will love him less, and that would make his situation worse.
So he puts up with any injustice, unkindness or cruelty in
the hope that one day his patience will be rewarded by
an increase in affection. But as time goes by and nothing
changes, anger and hate build up, and if it isn't expressed
it is turned inwards and leads to frustration and ultimately
to depression. Later in life this person is still incapble of
recognising his own needs, and even though he is now in
a position where he can fulfil his needs by choosing what

kind of people to associate with and by making sure that he is being treated lovingly and with respect, he cannot do so because he has never learned to respect himself. The firm belief that it is wrong to express anger leads to frustration and the attitude that you have to be grateful for what you get so that even the smallest amount of affection seems better than none.

FEAR OF AUTHORITY

Peter Pan withdraws into his Never-Never-Land to escape a world ruled by mothers and nannies, a world where children are made to follow instructions as set out by adults. In rebellion against the world of grown-ups, Peter gathers a group of boys around him and makes himself their leader, thus becoming himself a figure of authority who sets his own rules. Thanks to the dreamlike quality of Never-Never-Land, all runs smoothly and none of his little gang ever rebel against his leadership. Peter is the natural number one because only he possesses magic skills and therefore need not fear criticism or opposition; his special talents and abilities set him apart; he is the obvious hero in his world.

This is very much a child's way of looking at its parents. To a child's mind, parents are godlike creatures who are endowed with infinite knowledge, innumerable skills and magic powers. This is an understandable attitude when we remember that a young child has practically no knowledge, no skills and no powers of its own and must therefore necessarily be impressed by his elders. At this stage, the parents' authority is usually accepted, just as is Peter's authority with the other boys.

This illusion of omniscience and omnipotence will, however, be modified one day in the face of reality, and this is the process that never happens for Peter Pan. As children grow older and begin to acquire more knowledge, they begin to adjust their views about their parents, and this can be a painful process for both sides where the children lose some of their admiration and are no longer prepared to accept the parents' authority unquestioningly. Dad always told you that it is wrong to steal, and here he is producing a towel from your holiday resort from his suitcase. Mum always punished you for hitting your little brother when he wound you up, and here she is, hitting him herself because he is getting on her nerves. The child is not allowed to have a bar of chocolate in the supermarket, but the father treats himself to a packet of cigarettes. Children recognise these double standards and will point them out quite read-ily, much to the embarrassment of their parents. A lot depends now on how parents react to this criticism. They can punish the child for speaking out and tell it to shut up ('Mind your own business! Who are you to tell me how to behave!'), or they can make an excuse for having done what they shouldn't have done according to their own rules ('It was only a joke. Don't take everything so seriously!'; or 'If your brother cannot behave he'll have to bear the conse-quences.'), or they can admit that they have made a mis-take.

Many parents go for the first two options, trying to avoid the humiliation of having been caught out at doing the wrong thing. There is no way you can avoid losing your children's indiscriminate admiration in the course of time, but there is no need to lose their respect. Constantly pun-ishing children for criticising you and ridiculing their sense of justice does not help you save your face, it just creates hate. The stricter the rules parents impose on their children, the greater the disappointment when children discover their parents breaking these rules, and the harsher the children will judge their parents. When the rules leave no leeway to accommodate extraordinary circumstances, life becomes divided into right and wrong, black and white, good and bad, and it is very disturbing when this order is upset. Children's behaviour reflects the way they are treated by their parents; a person's attitude to authority reflects how his parents handled their position as authority figures.

A generalised hate of authority indicates that personal growth has come to a halt sometime during childhood or adolescence. When your ego is not sufficiently developed and you have no self-confidence, you feel that you have no control over what is happening to you. You feel at the bottom of the pecking order and at the mercy of everyone above you. This is a disturbing and frightening situation to be in and usually results in hate and disdain for your superiors. Even though you can now see that these superiors have their faults, you nevertheless fear their disapproval or punishment. Although you are frightened and would like to withdraw from situations where you are faced with an authority figure, you cannot really ever do so because wherever you go, whatever profession you are in, whatever sort of life you lead, you will every once in a while be confronted with people who are in a superior position to you. Because you have low self-esteem, you will automatically promote most other people into a position of authority. As you don't display any self-respect, others will treat you without respect, and this will then reinforce your attitude. A vicious circle is set into motion where your worst fears are confirmed by reality.

The way out of this dilemma is to start building up self-confidence and self-esteem by removing old emotional blocks, so that the way is cleared for learning new ways of dealing with others.

FEAR OF CHANGING TO A NEW PHASE

There are certain stages in life where we need to change from one role to another. Our social context changes and we make the transition from adolescent to adult, from single person to married person, from husband to father, and so on. Going into a new phase is usually a gradual process, and traditional rites of passage help ease us into the new role. Ceremonies such as engagements and weddings make the change-over an official one where it is publicly declared that a new phase is now beginning. In some religions there are similar ceremonies to make the transition from childhood to adolescence, for example the Jewish tradition of bar mitzvah where the young man is introduced as a full member into the religious community.

New phases bring with them new tasks and additional responsibilities and, above all, they alter the status that a person has in society. People look at you with different eyes, depending on whether you are a single woman, a mother of two or a mother of five. Their behaviour towards you will depend on their attitude towards, for example, single women. They may feel sorry for you because they consider being single a misfortune or some sort of under-achievement; others may envy you because they see you as having a great deal of freedom. Accordingly you will be encouraged or, as the case may be, discouraged when you announce plans of marriage.

Parents may find it very difficult to let their son move away from home and start his own family, and the pro-verbial dragon of a mother-in-law is entangled in precisely that situation. She cannot make the change from being a mother (and thereby number one in her son's life) to being a mother-in-law (and therefore number two). All the fault-finding with the daughter-in-law is just another way of saying to her son, 'You should not have left me because I'm still the best.' The mother is clinging to her old role and refuses to let go of it even though it has now become inappropriate since the situation has changed. When the son has been the focal point in her life, maybe even to the exclusion of other things, it is understandable that his going away creates great emotional upset, and yet the change-over needs to be effected eventually or the mother–son relationship, as well as the relationship between the newly-weds, can be seriously damaged.

It is the dread of losing a familiar life-style and all the positive emotions and rewards that go with it that makes people resist change. The mother-in-law worries about losing her son and being no longer needed; Peter Pan wor-ries about losing that sense of adventure and fun that he associates with being a child. They both base their negative outlook on the assumption that with the start of a new phase the old phase will have to be completely abandoned; but this is not so in reality. Even though some aspects change, others remain the same: the son is now more involved in his new family, but his love for his mother remains the same; Peter Pan leaves his Never-Never-Land, but his sense of adventure can direct him into a profession that fulfils his need for excitement and freedom. Rather than losing old companions, you are adding new ones. You can only have old friends when you go out and make new ones. The mother-in-law gains a daughter and she gains more leisure time to dedicate to the development of other interests, and this way she becomes a more interesting person who attracts the friendship of other people outside her immediate family.

PART III

12. AIMS OF PERSONAL DEVELOPMENT

IF YOU don't know where you are going, you can't get lost – but you won't arrive either. Not having an aim in life means not being able to select from the variety of choices life has to offer. You take what comes your way, but it doesn't have a meaning because you cannot put it into a personal framework. We sometimes go through phases where we are bored with everything we do, where nothing manages to arouse our interest: work is a slog, private life is dull, and there seems to be nothing to look forward to in the future.

The initial worries and hassles we had when we started in our present job are over, but so is the excitement and satisfaction of mastering new skills and achieving something productive. Knowing that we are able to deal with any possible problems easily, the job is no longer challenging and we begin to do it mechanically. We are on auto-pilot – and bored.

Being in a rut is of course not confined to work. It happens also in relationships and in the domestic environment. Partners can get bored with one another; a mother can feel exasperated with looking after her children day in day out; a voluntary helper can tire of the task he has set for himself. Visible outer signs for having reached that stage are letting yourself go, not caring about your appearance any more, and becoming stressed through the uniformity of what you are doing. Even though this sort of stress appears more benign than stress caused through being overworked, it nevertheless needs to be taken seriously as it can be just as soul-destroying to be underworked as it is being overworked.

It appears that, every once in a while, we outgrow the framework we have set for ourselves. When the novelty of our situation has worn off, this is usually followed by a period of contentment where we feel in control of what we are doing, knowing that we are doing our job well. How long this period lasts depends on each individual person: a few months for some, several years for others. When we finally outgrow this stage, the formerly useful structure we operated in becomes restrictive and hampers our personal growth.

The time has come when we have to reinvent our life and ourselves. We have to create new interests, new tasks for ourselves, or we are in danger of stagnating. It is a good idea to take charge of this developmental process and get it underway before you are forced to do so. Life around us changes constantly and, unless we go along with these changes, we are overtaken by them one day, and then we are pressurised into decisions that we never wanted to make. It is a bit like a growing family who leaves it to the last moment to find a bigger house. They may finally be so desperate for more space that in the end they pay more than they intended for a bigger place they don't really want.

On the other hand, rather than setting your own target and bringing about change through your own actions, you can sit back and wait for change to happen by itself. You can hope that, as circumstances around you change, your situation improves by itself. This is fine as long as you are content with the way things are. If you are unhappy, however, waiting for change (rather than promoting it) will be enervating and frustrating. And how long are you going to wait? Unless you set yourself a clear deadline and keep to it, waiting can become an excuse for inactivity.

Going for new aims, be they big or small, can be easier than you think, and it can be fun too. Why be boring when you can be interesting? Why be mediocre when you can be special? Find out what it is that makes you the unique individual that you are and reassess your priorities; generate new ideas and expand your strengths.

AIMS

There are times when we feel we could do more with our life, that our present situation is no longer fulfilling, even though there is nothing that causes us problems; work is OK, family life is OK, and yet. . . Often, these feelings are vague and we only sense a faint but constant dissatisfaction that pervades our daily routine, and not being able to put a finger on what exactly causes this discontent makes it even more difficult to deal with it. How much easier if the cause is clearly visible and we can tackle it head-on!

Coming to a dead-end like that is usually a signal that it is time to reassess your life. What have you achieved so far? Was it what you had always wanted for yourself? Usually there are quite a few ideas that you have not even begun to put into practice. If you are at a loss as to what it might be that could catch your imagination, think back to when you were between ten and twenty years of age. What were your dreams about yourself, your ambitions, your hopes? What were the things that fascinated you then, and what things did you find easy to do? Frequently, our true talents and interests are already apparent in adolescence; we just tend to forget about them later on in life because we are too busy walking down the well-worn paths of school, university, work, buying a car, a house, getting married and having children.

The beauty of self-development is that you don't need to produce a certificate or diploma at the end to know that you have benefited from it. New aims can consist of something useful and conventional, but they can equally well be frivolous, purely pleasurable and without any practical use to anyone. Any new knowledge you acquire, any new interest you get involved in, brings you further as a person and adds to your personality. By immersing yourself in new subjects you are opening a new world to yourself, and there is nothing so exhilarating and refreshing as being absorbed in an activity that holds your attention to the extent that you forget the world around you. Have you ever watched a stamp collector sitting over his books? It is like watching a child at play, totally absorbed. I'm not suggesting that you take up collecting stamps (unless this is what you have always wanted to do); it is the *involvement* in an activity rather than the activity itself which is important.

You may want to develop some of your strong points. If you are a good organiser you may want to get a neighbourhood crèche going, or you may want to set up a networking business. Your new aim may be another step up the career ladder, or it may be to do a course in calligraphy. Or you may want to learn how to swim or go on a survival trek in the mountains. The options are endless, and as you start looking for your personal area of interest you will discover a whole new set of ideas that you never knew existed.

So we are not talking about the 'right' or the 'wrong' aims; we are talking about new, about different ideas. Whatever aim is right for you may be unsuitable for the next person or even for the next hundred persons, but that doesn't make it wrong for you. Your aim is your personal choice and as such an expression of what makes you the person you are. By working on a new idea you give it meaning, and it is this meaningfulness that leads to the sense of fulfilment and satisfaction which we commonly call happiness.

RISKS

Undertaking a new venture can seem a risky business. You may have been away from formal schooling for twenty years and you may be worried about your ability to get back into the learning process. Will you be able to grasp new concepts? How are you going to cope with new technology such as electronic typewriters, word processors or computers? Will all the younger people overtake you because they are quicker on the uptake and more with it? Women who have left their job to raise a family are often faced with these sorts of doubts. The children have come to an age where they don't need full-time attention any more and there are gaps in the day that could be filled with something new and exciting, but by then you have not worked in your profession for quite a few years, and the prospect of returning to work suddenly appears a bit daunting. New methods may have been introduced since you left, and it is going to be 'back to school' for you. Bringing up children can be very rewarding, but it is also stressful, and the leap from domestic sphere and coping with young children to office environment and dealing with adults can seem a very long one!

Similar fears can arise even when you are already in a job and are sent on a course or decide to further your education by going to evening classes or taking a degree with the Open University. Going back into an active learning process puts you in a vulnerable position: you lay yourself open to failure. Whereas in your present job you can be fairly confident that you are more or less in control of what you are doing, with your new venture the outcome is much more uncertain.

How fearful you feel about your new venture will also partly depend on how you fared in your schooldays. If you had an unpleasant time at school being punished or ridiculed by either teachers or parents, you are less likely to want to take the risk of going back into a similar situation; and if you do, you will feel more anxious than someone who can look back on happy school memories.

A different type of risk occurs when you decide that you need to change jobs because your present job is too stressful or underpaid or both. It takes insight and self-confidence to make such a decision and not feel inferior because you cannot cope with a crazy workload. Many people feel a failure when they are unable to conquer an ever-increasing mountain of work; if you can accept that it is not a shortcoming in yourself but rather a feature of the particular job you are in, then it is a constructive move to look elsewhere for a more reasonable job. The risk in making that move is that a nagging little doubt may remain that maybe, after all, you were not competent enough or that other people may think you were not competent enough to cope and that you are running away. The best way of avoiding that risk is to ask yourself a few questions:

*are there other people in your department who are over-loaded with work?;

*is your workload such that you couldn't finish it even if you did overtime regularly?;

*have you asked to get someone in to help you take some of the work off your hands, and this has not been possible?;

*do you feel that your health/well-being/private life is negatively affected by your work?

If you have answered 'yes' to even only one of the above questions, and if the overload situation has been going on over a prolonged period of time, it is likely that stress is an inherent property of your job, in which case you need to take responsibility for your own well-being and leave that unwholesome situation.

In an extreme case you may even want to change your professional direction altogether, and that entails maybe the highest risk of all. When you are used to a certain income and your standard of living is adapted to your present salary, there can be great financial obstacles to leaving your job. You have most probably made financial commitments which are based on your present salary. Should you now decide to go into a very different profession it is more than likely that you will have to retrain which means that there are not only course fees to pay but also a loss of income while you are retraining, unless you can get your qualifications by correspondence or in evening and weekend-courses.

That is why any radical career changes need to be thought through very carefully before you take any steps such as handing in your notice, or you will end up replacing stress at work with the stress of having no income. If you really want to change then you will find a viable way, but it may not be easy. It will require sacrifices on your part, you may have to give up free time and a lot of your social life, as well as a lot of financial comforts. On the other hand, you cannot avoid pitfalls by never taking a chance. The world around us is changing all the time, and by doing nothing we may be taking the greatest risk of all.

APPROACH

As we have seen, you may experience some doubts before you can launch your new plan, but once you have dealt with them you are ready to take the first steps.

Your approach will depend largely on your personality and on the way you operate; the way you achieve your aim will be an individual one. There is no such thing as a 'right' or a 'wrong' method of going about transforming ideas into reality; there are only a great variety of different ways, some of which will work for you and others of which won't. Bear in mind that if you cannot make headway in one direction there are still other roads to your aim that you can take. Just keep your mind firmly fixed on your aim while you are dealing with the more mundane aspects of getting there; hang on to your dreams and don't be put off by setbacks, and you are bound to succeed.

Decide

Initially, make sure that you know exactly what you are aiming for. Write down your aim clearly and in detail. Be specific about what you want. Don't just say, 'I want to learn how to dance', but identify what sort of dancing you mean: are you interested in ballroom dancing, rock 'n' roll or breakdancing? Don't just say you want to get out of your old job, think about what sort of new job you want. Do you want more responsibility, more scope, more variety, more money? Or are you looking for a job that entails less travelling or shorter hours so that you have more time for your family or your hobbies?

Being precise about your aim makes it easier for you to recognise an opportunity when it comes your way. As long as you are vague about what you want you will walk straight past your ideal job or pastime simply because you are not mentally switched on.

Once your aim is clearly defined in your mind, write it down on a piece of paper and put it somewhere where you will see it every day. Let the note help remind you of what it is you are trying to achieve. Show yourself that you mean business, that you are heading for success.

Set yourself an initial date to check on interim results. Once you are clear about what it is you want, make a note in your diary for a review of your progress in two weeks' time. What have you achieved? Have you taken active steps towards your aim? Can you see any results yet? Work out a course of action for the immediate future and take one step at a time.

Prepare

Before you begin on your new venture there is usually a lot of groundwork to be done. You have to find out who offers the course you want and possibly compare several different institutions. You will have to deal with a certain amount of administrational work as you enrol and you may have to arrange for someone to look after the children while you are out. If you have finally decided to build that shelving system for your living room, you may need to get reference books from the library, borrow or buy the appropriate tools and obtain all the materials.

Be methodical about your preparation; this will save you time in the long run. Make a list of things you need to do and tick items off as you go along. Careful preparation saves a lot of hassle once you start with your task. Also, sitting down and actually writing things down forces you to think clearly about what you need to do, and that helps you focus your attention on the next step.

If you are thinking of setting up your own business, your preparation has to include a detailed business plan as well as market research. As you may have to borrow money from the bank to get started, you will be required to demonstrate the soundness of your business idea anyway, so you may as well think your project through thoroughly straight from the beginning. Enthusiasm and a good product idea are *not* enough to make a business viable. Tools, premises, advertising and marketing cost money – always more than you think. A high percentage of businesses fold within the first year, and many do not see the end of the second year, not because their product is not good but because the financial commitments were higher than the owner expected. It is therefore essential to get expert advice *before* you invest any money. Choosing the wrong evening class is one thing, paying off a bankloan for a business that has gone bankrupt is another. Do not overstretch yourself financially. When you are running your own business you will need your holidays, and they cost money too!

Taking the plunge

Get started NOW! You have invested too much mental and emotional energy to abandon your project now. Whenever you get worried about whether you are going to succeed, think of someone who has already achieved what you are attempting at the moment. If they can do it, you can do it too; and don't think for a moment that they got where they are now without any problems. An achiever is someone who has conquered his doubts, who was determined and inspired enough to go on when things got difficult.

Use obstacles constructively. If you find it difficult to stick to your diet because you see food lying around in the kitchen, use this opportunity to tidy up your cupboards, throw out old stuff and put all foods away and out of sight. When you have problems finding a babysitter so that you can attend your evening class, negotiate with a neighbour or friend to have your kids over for one night and offer to have her children over in return on another night. That way everyone has gained something, including the children, who will find it exciting to stay away from home overnight.

PROGRESS

If you find that your plan doesn't run as smoothly as you had hoped, it doesn't mean that your plan is no good, it just means that you may have to spend some time on either ironing out the fault or working your way around it. It does *not* mean that you have to abandon the entire plan. Flexibility and imagination are of great help in such a situation because they will allow you to look at the problem from different angles.

When you have set up your business and done absolutely everything that you can and then are waiting for the first orders to roll in, you can either despair about only getting one enquiry per day, or you can say to yourself that this is the time to read some good books or finish knitting that jumper because once your business flourishes, you won't have time for these things. Or make use of your time by learning how to relax physically and mentally – this will come in handy in stressful situations when you want to keep a cool head.

Once you have launched your new project it is essential to keep a tab on how you are doing as you go along. Set aside specific times to review your progress and to check whether things are still going according to plan. If they are not, you may want to revise your strategy accordingly.

How you rate your progress will, of course, depend on your expectations. Be patient with yourself. It will take time for development to show. It is unreasonable to expect to understand the late night French film without looking at the subtitles when you have only been to French classes for three weeks; and there is no point in stepping on the scales six hours after you have started your new diet. When you haven't lost all your excess pounds by the time you reach your deadline, don't give up! Losing weight slowly is much healthier than shedding it too quickly. Your plan to get down to your ideal weight is still good, as long as you have lost *some* weight by the appointed time. This is the point where many people give up ('Oh well, no point, I can't do it; I might as well eat what I like!') when all that happened was that their expectations didn't match reality. So you only lost half the weight you were hoping to lose within your time limit; rather than deploring the slowness of your metabolism, acknowledge how well you have done up until now. It takes determination and perseverance to stick to a diet, and you have just demonstrated that you have these qualities. Well done! Now take a deep breath and dive into the second half of your task. If you could master the first half, you can master the second half too.

Don't ignore small steps of progress: a collection of small

steps makes a staircase in the end! Maybe we all expect development to be a more obvious affair where each and every one of our efforts is noisily rewarded and acknowledged by people around us, when more often than not the contrary is the case. The struggling non-smoker is told, 'Why don't you have a cigarette? At least you'll be in a better mood again!'; the enthusiastic student of Italian architecture is asked why he didn't pick an evening class in plumbing instead so that he could finally fix the toilet. The aspiring businesswoman hears gloomy forecasts by worried relatives and friends that her idea is not going to work. Strangely enough, these are the same people that will go around telling everyone they always knew you had it in you once you have succeeded. . .

When you are dissatisfied with the way things are going you need to stop and think the situation over, but remember that criticism alone is counterproductive unless it is followed by action. Most of the time you have more control than you think over the way your plans progress.

To keep your motivation up while you are pursuing your aim, spend some time every day imagining having achieved your aim. Close your eyes and visualise yourself in all those everyday situations without a cigarette in your hand and imagine how proud you will feel; imagine yourself in France, having a conversation with the inhabitants of your holiday village and applying your knowledge of French; spend time imagining your business flourishing and yourself managing it easily and effortlessly, reaping the well-deserved fruits of your labour. This type of day-dreaming is particularly important in times when progress seems slow or blocked and when you come close to giving up. It is at times like these when you need to have a vision of what you are trying to achieve, an image that will pull you through and give you the strength to carry on and win in the end.

13. STRATEGIES OF OPTIMISM

HOW TO STAY OPTIMISTIC WHEN THINGS GO WRONG

WHEN a problem holds up the flow of progress we are often only too ready to doubt ourselves, doubt the validity of our aim, and doubt the successful outcome of our enterprise. Unexpected events that interfere with our routine are a threat to our stability. We overreact, and it is precisely this feeling of panic that prevents us from solving the problem as quickly as possible. It is not the problem itself that shakes our self-confidence – it is our own attitude towards the problem that prevents us from tackling the obstacle quickly and efficiently.

Some time ago I observed a big boy being bullied by another boy half his size. It seemed incredible that this could happen, considering that the big boy could have just shoved his adversary aside with one movement; and yet, he allowed the small boy to kick him and push him about. Maybe he thought he couldn't or shouldn't defend himself for some reason, or maybe he thought he deserved to be treated like that. The fact remains that his attitude was such that he was unable to use his assets to solve his problem of being bullied.

When we panic as soon as things go wrong we are doing a similar thing: we undermine our own ability to solve the problem. As soon as we perceive a danger signal on our way we freeze, decide we cannot cope with it and run away, abandoning all; in other words, we do not fulfil our potential. If we believe that we are ruled by forces outside our control (for example, the bully), we are likely to act accordingly. If, however, we believe in our power to direct events we can become active and make our ideas reality. We need to be *aware* of our own strength in order to have it at our disposal in an emergency.

Every problem has its weak point, and that is where you

can drive in the wedge to get rid of it; but before you can get rid of the difficulty you will have to face it. Running away from it is only a short-term relief. Turn around and look at what is bothering you and holding you up. You will find that the problem is only half as bad as you thought. Dissect the problem into all its details and disentangle it in order to find a solution, and you will notice how the problem loses its hold over you. By looking at your obstacle you assume control over the situation, and that makes it less of a threat. As you are breaking the problem down into small manageable parts you can deal with them one by one and dismantle the entire structure with a minimum of effort and fear.

Your three major steps for keeping up your spirits in a difficult situation are therefore

observing – deciding – acting.

Let us look at some examples. One day you notice that a colleague at work is very short with you; she appears to be upset. You wonder what is the matter and whether you have done something to annoy her, so you start observing how this colleague behaves towards other people. Is she unfriendly with everyone or just with you? Depending on how you assess her behaviour you will have to decide what you want to do. If your colleague is hostile towards you alone, you can either stay out of her way and wait until the storm has passed (non-action), or you can ask her what the matter is (action). Depending on how stable your self-confidence is, you will go for the non-action or the action plan. If you find, on the other hand, that your colleague is equally short with everyone, you can again choose between two options: if you feel indifferent towards her, you may want to ignore her for a while (non-action), or, if you are interested in her or in a pleasant atmosphere in the office, you may want to approach her and discover the reason for her bad mood (action).

Most of the time we choose non-action rather than action because we are afraid of what we might find out. Instead of asking, we give ourselves a hard time by conjuring up all sorts of things we might have done to offend the other person. Rather than finding out the truth we torture ourselves with nightmarish self-accusations; in other words we resort to mental overdrive and create anxieties for ourselves.

Or take the following case. The boiler of your central heating system suddenly makes frighteningly loud noises when you switch it on. The system is quite new and has only been installed two years ago. You call the central heating company and when the engineer arrives he tells you that the pump needs replacing and that you will have to pay for it because your first year guarantee has expired. He also mentions that the pump has probably broken down because of the faulty placing of a vent during installation of the system. The engineer advises you that, unless this vent is replaced, the chances are that your new pump will soon be ruined too. He installs the new pump and asks you to pay for it, which you may well do.

By this stage your are probably fuming. Not only did you have to pay for a repair that was caused by faulty installation in the first place, but you also have to expect a second bill if you want to avoid further damage to the system; a truly annoying situation. So what can you do?

As always you have a number of options. You can either rant and rave and tell all your friends and neighbours about the injustice of it all, or you can sit down for a moment and think about it. Look at the facts calmly. The central heating company have made a mistake but expect you to pay for it because the system is no longer under guarantee. It is unlikely that the company will offer to do the repairs for free unless you ask for it; therefore you need to decide whether you want to go on being upset (non-action) or whether you prefer trying to do something about it (action). If you go for the active option, you would have to write a letter to the company's director, explaining what has happened and asking for the free installation of a new vent as well as a refund of the money you paid out for the new pump. If you have paid by cheque, you may want to tell your bank to cancel it.

You observe what is happening, you then assess where the point of attack needs to lie and make a decision, and finally you put your idea for a solution into practice. The more often you practice this sort of approach successfully, the greater your belief in your own strength will become, and this will finally result in a feeling of self-reliance and optimism that is based on having successfully mastered previous complications.

Taking a constructive attitude towards difficulties increases the range of possibilities available to you because the better you get at solving small problems the greater the likelihood of you coping with bigger ones. By learning to deal with adverse situations you extend the boundaries of your awareness of possible experiences and actions, and you are truly on your way to becoming your own person.

Remove obstacles and forget them. You can do anything you really want to do, you *can* overcome difficulties, and in the process you will get to know yourself, your own abilities, and your power to achieve things.

HOW TO STAY OPTIMISTIC WHEN SURROUNDED BY PESSIMISTIC PEOPLE

It is a well-known fact that one grumpy person can mar the atmosphere in an entire office or department. A bad-tempered secretary radiates discord and conflict around her and others will pick up on it. Before you know it, the air is heavy with pessimism and hopelessness, and you catch it like the common cold.

Even though you may realise that you are not responsible for your colleague's mood, it can be difficult to dissociate yourself sufficiently to avoid contagion.

Let us look at the situation from a different viewpoint. Remember the last time you were in a bad mood. What was it that helped you get out of it? Did you just snap out of it yourself or did someone else come to the rescue? When you are disgruntled, how do you want other people to behave towards you so that you can feel better again?

It is usually a kind word from someone else that makes you stop in your tracks and relax. When someone is prepared to give you some time and listen to you, you tend to unwind and get things back into proportion. Feeling that someone else cares enough about you to ask you whether you are OK is therapeutic in itself. Nobody *wants* a bad mood and disharmony, not even the person who creates it; it is therefore pointless to treat that person as if they were doing it on purpose.

You may find it daunting to approach a bad-tempered friend, but ignoring him or her is not a solution either because that makes the other person feel even worse. Even though your friend may shout 'Nothing!' at the top of his voice when you ask him what the matter is, don't let that discourage you. Bear in mind that the harsh reaction you are getting is a measure of how unhappy your friend is. Some people need to be talked to in a friendly way for a while until they come out of their shell, others will respond more quickly to your endeavours.

Showing genuine kindness can be of great help to someone who is displaying signs of downheartedness. You can give moral support by pointing out the other person's good points and thereby helping them to think more positively about themselves. It is important to be truthful in your praise, though; there is no point in complimenting someone dishonestly. However, you can certainly encourage someone by acknowledging their efforts to improve and change for the better.

A little girl who shares her sweets with her brother, however reluctantly, is more likely to share again if she is praised for it. The attitude of 'It's about time you did that!' is negative and implies that the child's efforts are only just sufficient to please the parents, that they are nothing special. Positive encouragement creates an atmosphere of acceptance and understanding and this makes it easier for people to overcome their weaknesses and change for the better.

Make it a point of duty to pass on complimentary remarks; gossip constructively, not destructively. We have a tendency to repeat only sensational bits of news, and they tend to be negative. Let's turn this around and create euphoria rather than gloom and doom. As discussed earlier in the book, negative news is only part of reality and cannot give us a representative picture of life. By shifting our attention to the positive sides we generate good-will and happiness, and all of a sudden life appears in a more positive light. Let's home in on the silver lining in close-up! Life is too short to waste it on pessimism.

GETTING CONTROL OF YOUR EMOTIONS AND YOURSELF

In my hypnotherapy practice I treat people who suffer from various emotional problems such as depression, anxiety, phobias, lack of self-confidence, migraines, stuttering, eating disorders and other conditions where the psychological equilibrium is upset. The cause for these emotional imbalances lies either in events that occurred in childhood or in one or several traumatic incidents in the more recent past. Ordinarily, an upsetting event is dealt with, consciously or subconsciously, over a period of time until it has been worked through sufficiently to be 'filed away' in the mind. When someone near and dear to you dies, you go through a number of phases such as disbelief, grief, anger and remorse, until you get over the loss and are able to behave in your usual manner and enjoy life again. When you have been mugged or burgled you will need weeks to recover from the shock and months to get back to your old self, but even then these events leave scars. Even though you take all sorts of precautions like carrying an alarm or fitting your doors and windows with extra locks, you still feel unsafe and emotionally disturbed by what happened for quite some time.

When a traumatic event is so unbearable that it threatens our very existence, a person will repress that memory so that it appears that the event never happened. This is an internal defence mechanism that ensures that someone can continue existing, however badly, rather than go mad because of what happened to him or her.

When I speak of 'unbearable' events then this has to be seen in relative terms. Incidents that are anxiety-inducing to one child may not have the same effect on another child; circumstances that are intolerable to a child may be easy for an adult to deal with. The extent to which a person is shocked by misfortune depends on personality and personal circumstances at the time, and consequently repression may or may not occur.

But even though an unpleasant memory is repressed, the emotions accompanying the event at the time are still there and will create internal pressure, and this pressure needs to be relieved. Either the pressure is directed outside and expresses itself as anger or aggression, or it is directed inwards and manifests itself as depression or anxiety, either as anxiety that is free-floating, where the person is unaware of what is sparking off the panic attack, or anxiety that is linked to a specific object, for example lifts, heights, birds, open spaces and so on.

In cases where past events hinder personal development and growth, it is necessary to find the root cause of that block, and that may need to be done professionally. A qualified hypnotherapist who has had training in psychoanalysis would be one way of working through the past and bringing repressions to light so that they can be dealt with. Hypnosis is an invaluable tool to bring suppressed subconscious material to the surface. Once repressions have been brought to conscious awareness they can be worked through in an appropriate adult way and they can then become part of the person's conscious memory bank. In this way, negative emotions linked up with the repressed events can be set free and dispersed. People who have gone through analysis and released a repression often experience the liberating emotional effects immediately in that they find that they don't get upset that easily any more. It is like removing a prop from the spout of a kettle so that the steam can escape. Once the steam has an outlet, the kettle won't have to explode or implode.

Paradoxically, the only way to control your emotions is to let them out. The more forceful you are in suppressing negative feelings, the more powerful they become and the greater their hold over you. It is of course not always possible or socially acceptable to express your emotions, on the contrary. It can be professionally disadvantageous if you fly off the handle too easily, just as it can be a stumbling block to your career if you are too timid and can't say no. In a social setting, controlling your anger is considered more important than controlling your anxiety. Someone who is angry is a lot less acceptable than someone who is shy. Strangely enough, both behaviours, although they seem opposed, go back to the same root, namely fear. A person who explodes is a person who allows resentment to build up, and that means that he has not had the courage to deal with small annoying events as and when they cropped up. The inability to tackle upsetting issues head-on as and when they occur allows grievances to accumulate and grow into a bundle of dynamite which is ignited by the smallest spark. The only difference between the aggressive person and the shy one is that the aggressive person explodes whereas the shy one implodes, with the latter reaction leading to depression in extreme cases.

Although professional help is advised in some cases, there are certainly some things you can learn and achieve for yourself. The main thing is that you start with *small* tasks. The only way you can fail is by taking steps that are too big. If you are shy and find it difficult to speak to people, it is too daunting to make an evening in the local disco your first objective. It is much more sensible to start with people you know, people who you are reasonably sure like you. Set yourself the aim of addressing them first when you see them next time rather than wait for them to start talking to you. Ask them for a small favour, utter your own opinion in a cautious way. Once you are at ease with these small tasks (which initially may well seem big tasks) you can go on to a more difficult level. Attempting something that is too far removed from your present level of abilities induces too much fear and self-consciousness and is therefore more likely to fail.

At a more advanced level, you need to learn to lose your fear of conflict. Many people will do anything to avoid a row, even if it means having to abandon their own wishes and aspirations. They cannot bear raised voices or hysterical outbursts when they see them happen to others, let alone to themselves, and just the thought of getting into an argument sends them into a panic.

It is good to be mild-mannered, as long as it is not an avoidance strategy. If you give in too often to other people's demands and wishes at the expense of your own you will begin to build up negative feelings such as resentment, anger and frustration. Begin to take your own needs seriously and start communicating them. A row often happens when two people have left it too late to speak to one another about their needs and now have to do so in an emotional manner. Make sure you negotiate your position at an early stage; that way you can do it in a matter-of-fact way. The longer you postpone announcing your wishes the more difficult it becomes for you to do so later on. It is ludicrous to let someone give you pea-soup every day when you hate pea-soup but don't dare say so out of politeness. The longer this goes on the more repulsive the soup becomes and the more embarrassed you are to say something about it – you are stuck with it.

We often expect events to be more dramatic than they turn out to be. We think that it will be a hard fight getting what we want. We get prepared to bash in doors, only to find that when we finally pluck up the courage, not only are the doors open but we also encounter a cooperative attitude at the other end. Very rarely do we encounter the resistance we expect. The problem seems worse while it is in our heads, where we allow it to grow out of all proportion.

Most of us have developed an expertise for pessimism, in spite of the facts that prove that *most* of our endeavours succeed. And yet, we are more impressed by *one* thing that goes wrong than by a *hundred* things that go right.

There is a lot we can do about attaining a more optimistic attitude (see also my book *Positive Thinking*), not only when we are of a timid disposition, but equally when we want to work on our short temper. If you get impatient with others quickly, chances are that you are someone who won't forgive himself if he makes mistakes. Ease up on yourself. Allow yourself breaks, take a step back, postpone an angry outburst for ten seconds. If you have to yell, at least sort out things afterwards when you have simmered down. Explain what it is you want and explain it clearly. Listen to what the other person has to say, and listen carefully. Working or living with other people is a process of negotiation, not a battle.

What are the things that annoy you? Do you explode

when someone calls you mean? If you do, it indicates that the other person has touched upon a sore point, and this usually means that you think there is truth in the accusation but are anxious not to look at that side of your personality too closely.

Begin to listen to your own feelings. Learn to take notice when you are beginning to feel uneasy and check the situation immediately. What is it that makes you feel edgy? Observe your feelings, assess the situation and do something about it while you are still relatively calm.

No matter how guilty you think the other party is, do not accuse or point the finger. Remember that every time you point a finger, there are three fingers pointing back at you. Accusing others can easily lead to an escalation of conflict and it could also prove embarrassing for you when you find out that the suspicions you had were unfounded. . .

Assertiveness courses teach a method which is very useful in this context, and that is to begin your sentences with 'I' rather than with 'you'. 'You' sentences, as in 'You always forget to lock the door!' and 'You never take me to the theatre!', are accusatory, whereas 'I am annoyed that I just found the door unlocked again' and 'I'd really like to go to the theatre with you' are much more likely to get a positive response.

Angry outbursts frighten people around you, and although angry demands are often fulfilled, they are only fulfilled grudgingly. Aggression results in fear and hate of the aggressor because it corners the other person without giving him the possibility of negotiating his position.

It is perfectly acceptable to declare that you are not satisfied with the way a colleague treats you or with the way your project group works. What is unacceptable is to yell your head off as you say it. Help yourself by building up more self-confidence, tackling small things to start with. If you need help with it, find out about courses on communication skills or assertiveness training.

When your anger has built to an extent where you need to release it one way or another, you may want to try the following exercise once you are away from the frustrating situation or person.

The Anger Room

– Sit or lie down and close your eyes. Take a deep breath and get ready to get *really* angry.

– Imagine yourself at the bottom of a flight of stairs with ten steps. Begin to walk up the steps and get angrier as you do so.

– At the top, find yourself in front of a black door which has a sign on it that says ANGER ROOM. Reach out your hand, turn the door handle, open the door and feel yourself stepping inside the room. Close the door behind you. Now you find yourself in a room that is filled with secondhand china, glassware, porcelaine, figurines and other fragile pieces.

– Let your anger out now, and start breaking every single piece of crockery in sight. Smash it on the floor, trample on it (of course you are wearing heavy duty shoes!), jump on it, and imagine yourself yelling and shouting as you do so. When you have completely demolished the contents of the entire room, sit down for a rest and look around you. Notice a second door in the room which has a sign on it that reads SOLUTION ROOM.

– Walk over to that door and open it. Enter the Solution Room and see an ordinary table in the room with two chairs either side. On one chair sits the person whose actions upset you.

– Walk across the room and take a seat in the other chair. Begin to speak to the other person by saying, 'I would like to comment on what has been happening today/recently. I feel . . .' and continue to speak about all your grievances in great detail, but calmly. As you are speaking, imagine your partner remaining silent, but listening attentively to what you are saying.

– When you have finished, walk to a third door which is marked RELAXATION, open it and begin to walk down a flight of stairs with ten steps. Imagine yourself getting more and more relaxed the further down you get, glad that you got things off your chest.

14. STRATEGIES AS TOOLS

LEARN HOW TO DO NOTHING

You may ask yourself what a chapter on 'doing nothing' is doing in a book on personal development. Surely, self-development means action, motion, energy and dynamics! Yes, it does, and the active component is probably the most widely publicised feature; and yet, it is only *one* aspect. Nobody can be active and energetic all day long, nobody can whizz around in overdrive on a permanent basis.

Not doing anything may sound like the easiest thing in the world, but to some people it is practically impossible. They are unable to leave a piece of work unfinished, they cannot bring themselves to take a break from a demanding job, and it is unthinkable for them to delegate part of their task to someone else. The mere thought of sitting down idly will produce a rush of anxiety that forces them to try and find something that still needs to be attended to. If you find this description exaggerated, let me assure you that this is a very real problem for quite a few people nowadays, and it is managers just as much as housewives who suffer from this compulsive activity-drive.

The problem often starts when the person goes through a particularly stressful time in their life, for example when a relative falls severely ill and requires round-the-clock care, or when the company structure changes all of a sudden and your job is on the line. Other stressful situations are when you have to cope with both a job and a family, or when you are working in an unfriendly environment where people are hostile or unhelpful. In these circumstances people will mobilise all their strength to pull themselves through and to overcome physical or emotional fatigue; they are, in other words, functioning on overdrive. We all have that resource within us to help us handle unusually demanding tasks, but this resourse is not inexhaustible.

Because stress and its negative side-effects creep up on

us gradually, it is difficult to judge when you can't take any more or when you need to take a break from it all. We tend to ignore the physical warning signals we get, such as headaches, fatigue or insomnia, and the stronger our sense of duty the more easily we will brush aside signs of strain.

A clear indication that you are overworked or under emotional pressure is when you find yourself paying inordinate attention to detail and trying to do everything at once. When your host gets the duster out and gives the window-sills the once over after having served the drinks; when a .colleague at work gets in a tizz because she is trying to dictate a letter, make a phonecall and tidy her desk all at the same time; when you come home after work, exhausted, and still feel you need to clear up and hoover your entire flat before you can go to sleep, then the line between drive and overdrive has already been overstepped. Another warning signal is unusually high sensitivity to noise.

When this compulsion to overwork is not checked in time, you run down your energy reserves and sooner or later you are running on empty, and that is when serious health problems start. A nervous breakdown is a classic example of stress overload.

As mentioned earlier, it is the conscientious type of personality with a strong sense of duty who is particularly prone to slipping into this habit of taking too much on board. In spite of the fact that the original cause of stress has long since gone, the routine is kept up because the person cannot allow him- or herself to wind down and thus recoup lost energy.

Overworking yourself is really a symptom that is produced by an inability to take yourself seriously. It is laudable if you don't complain about every little indisposition, but it is foolhardy to disregard constant physical or emotional discomfort. Lack of insight and insufficient knowledge about your own physical limits are the result of an upbringing where the child is faced with high demands and emotionally pressurised to perform exceptionally well in order to gain the parents' approval. When the parents are difficult to please, this can turn into a catch-22 situation where the child can never do quite enough to satisfy the parents. This is the origin of the desperate zeal to work extra hard in order to be liked or respected by others. The fact that you could be liked for your own person does not occur to workaholics because that was not the case with their parents.

Not everyone will be able to free themselves from this habit of compulsive activity, and often professional help is needed to work through the past so that the person is free to choose new attitudes. There are, however, quite a few positive steps you can take to regain control over your life, and these are outlined in the step-by-step guide at the end of this chapter.

Putting yourself back in charge of your activity levels means that you learn to make time for yourself, to step back from your tasks and create little islands of recreation that enable you to catch your breath and that ultimately help you preserve your health. Once you have run down your energy level too far it takes a long time to get it back to normal – months and possibly years in severe cases; so the sooner you can start to learn how to do nothing (and enjoy it!) the better.

STEP-BY-STEP GUIDE

STEP 1
Questionnaire

Ask yourself the following:

a) Who are you trying to please by working so hard?

    your parents
    your boss
    your colleages
    your husband/wife
    your children
    the church
    the taxman
    yourself?

b) What have the following people done recently to please you?

> your parents
> your boss
> your colleagues
> your husband/wife
> your children
> the church
> the taxman
> you?

If the second question seems peculiar to you, why do you think that is? Are you so busy doing other people favours that you have forgotten that you yourself have the right to be treated with consideration too? Or won't you allow other people to help you?

c) Have your recently rejected help that was offered to you? If so, was that because

– you think it doesn't count unless you do it all yourself?
– you don't trust others to do things properly?
– you don't want to admit that you can't cope?

Please take the time to consider seriously each of the above reasons. There are times in your life when you are snowed under with work, when you need to deal with so many things that it is impossible for one person to do it all. It is a sign of intelligence, rather than weakness, to let someone else help you. It is a sign of intelligence to carefully ration your strength, rather than working yourself into the ground. When you are sick in bed you are no good to anyone, so you are better off letting someone else take at least part of the burden off your shoulders.

When you delegate work you may well find that the job doesn't get done to your standards, and this is possibly one reason why you feel reluctant to let someone else do it. However, in a work overload situation there is no room for perfectionism. You will have to set your priorities, retain the work that is most important to you and give away those parts of the job that are less critical. This is what is called management, whether you head a company, a department or a family. The rules stay the same: you can't have one person do all the work. The manager's job is to manage, and that includes delegation.

STEP 2
Take breaks.

Allocate times in your schedule that are reserved for a break. Stick to your breaks as stubbornly as you do to your work. They are just as important.

STEP 3
Assess your health.

Do you suffer frequently from
– colds
– headaches
– upset stomach
– nervous bowel syndrome
– indigestion
– diarrhoea
– palpitations
– nausea
– dizziness
– exhaustion?

If you have problems with more than one of these conditions, your body is giving you a warning signal. Please take it seriously. Have a professional check-up, and if no organic cause can be established, your stress level is too high and you need to cut down.

Begin to listen to your body and stop pushing yourself over the limit.

STEP 4
Remind yourself to slow down.

Write yourself a note that says, 'Working without a break is inefficient and dangerous for my health and therefore detrimental to my personal development'. Read the note several times a day.

STEP 5

Learn to relax.

There are several options. The easiest is probably to go out and buy a walkman and a relaxation tape with either gentle music or a narrative of pleasant imagery on it.

Relaxing doesn't necessarily mean that your mind has to be totally blank. Ideally you would be able to achieve this after a lot of practising, but it is not really that essential. It is perfectly OK for you to be thinking while you are relaxing, *as long as it is about something pleasant*. Not thinking about anything at all is very difficult, and it can be discouraging when you have made time for a break and find that you feel totally frustrated at the end of it just because you could not stop thoughts from coming into your mind.

Here is an exercise which is easy to do and helps you to physically relax quickly.

RELAXATION EXERCISE

– Uncross your arms and legs. Put your feet flat on the ground.
– Begin to listen to the outside sounds, the cars in the street, noises next door, planes overhead etc.
– Bring your mind inside your room and begin to concentrate on the way you are sitting in your chair. Be aware of where your head is, your arms, your hands, the trunk of your body, your legs, your feet. Don't move your body; just think of those parts as you concentrate on them.
– Begin to tense your feet, hold the tension for a moment, then let go again. Do the same with your legs, your belly, your chest muscles, your hands and arms, your shoulders and your facial muscles (clench your teeth and frown).
– Begin to concentrate on your hands. Feel all the sensations in your hands: the warmth, the slight tingling in the palms of your hands, the throb of your pulsebeat.
– Imagine a huge barometer in front of you which is marked from ten to zero, ten being tension, zero being sleep, with all the various degrees of relaxation in between.
– Take a deep breath through your belly, and as you breathe out imagine the barometer dropping to eight. Take a deep

breath and watch the barometer fall further as you breathe out.

Repeat this process until you see the barometer as being down to two.

– Now begin to visualise the number 999. Begin to count backwards, visualising each number as you do so. As you go along, make the numbers progressively smaller and fainter until you cannot see the next number any more.

– When there are no more numbers, take your mind back to your barometer. See it on two.

– Then take your attention back to your hands and feel the pulse beating in your palms.

– Gently tense all the muscles in your body, and as you release then, open your eyes again.

Practise this exercise daily. The more you practise the better you are going to get at relaxing, and you will be able to do it more quickly. It is a useful skill to have and can also help you go to sleep in the evenings: just bring the barometer down to zero and don't tense up at the end.

Learning to do nothing is in itself an achievement and as such part of self-development. But you can also use it as a means to an end, to help you cope better with achieving your aims or your professional ambitions. The more work is involved in pursuing your plans, the more important it is to create a counterbalance to work pressure.

LEARN TO DO WHAT YOU WANT TO DO

Try and establish whether what you are doing is really what you want to do, rather than what you should do. When you feel that you are doing what you *should* do, you are implying that someone else has made the choice for you, or that you are doing something because you think someone else expects this of you.

Another way of not doing what you really want to do is to pursue something to spite someone else. I had a client some time ago who suffered from anxiety attacks. During analysis it came out that Derek (not his real name) had had a troubled relationship with his mother and with women in general. He felt that his mother was overbearing and oppressive, and he resented how, during his childhood, she had pushed his father around. He swore that this was not going to happen to him when he started seeing girls, so he in turn started to become domineering with women. On the one hand, Derek despised his father for being so weak, and on the other hand he hated his mother for the power she wielded over both his father and himself. His only defence against his mother and his only means of establishing himself as a person in his own right was to oppose his mother in whatever she said, no matter what. This became so important to him that he would frequently defy his mother even though he thought she was right.

When he was eighteen he went out with his first girl-friend, and although the relationship was good, Derek realised that it was not good enough to lead to marriage. One day, his mother commented that she didn't think it would be a good idea for Derek to get married to this girlfriend – so Derek decided he was going to get married as soon as possible, just to show that he was man enough to do anything he liked. Needless to say, the marriage didn't work out.

And so the story went on. Even though Derek had long left the parental home, he still acted as his mother's son. Whenever there was a decision to be made, he thought what his mother would decide and then went and did the exact opposite. Without him realising it, his mother was still ruling his entire life which was what he had always tried to avoid.

However, the problem with his rebellious approach was that Derek soon began to feel out of control because very often he was acting against his own better judgement. Having to compulsively oppose something he really wanted to do created unbearable conflicts for him that led to the massive panic attacks he suffered. Once he had understood why he was behaving as he did he was able to change his attitude gradually and make sure he got what he wanted, even though his mother might approve of his choice! His panic attacks vanished within a few weeks.

When it comes to our jobs, not all of us are in the lucky position of being in a profession that suits our talents or our temperament, so that we can say the job is really 'us'. To have a vocation, that is an occupation that you fill with heart and soul, is the ultimate example of doing what you want to do. You feel sure of what you are doing, confident that you can handle any problems that might arise in the course of your working day, and work and play seem to become one.

As we all have to go out and earn a living to pay the rent, the bills and, alas, the taxman, we cannot afford to hang around and wait for a vocation to come our way. What we can do, however, is to fill our free time with something that is important to us, no matter how trivial it may appear to others.

STEP-BY-STEP GUIDE

STEP 1

Collect ideas.

– Make a list of all those things you have always wanted to do but never got round to doing.
– Stop and think about your childhood dreams, about what you wanted to be when you grew up.
– Establish which are the things in life that come easily to you – except spending money.
– Imagine you were given a financial fortune so that you could buy anything you liked and didn't have to work ever again. Once you had bought everything you wanted, gone on all the holidays you wanted, what would you occupy the rest of your life with?

STEP 2

Assess your present situation concerning your job.

– Did you choose it yourself because it appealed to you?
– Did you choose it because it was expected of you?
– Did someone else choose it for you, for example your parents?

– Are you happy in your job, notwithstanding whether the choice was your own or someone else's?

It is not necessarily a bad thing if someone else gave you the idea of going into your present job. Sometimes, other people can point us in the right direction, assessing quite accurately what is suitable for us. But there is still the possibility that they are wrong, and it is important for us to be aware of that possibility and check against our own feelings whether we approve of the suggested direction.

What I would like you to do in this Step is to look critically at what your position is. We rarely stop and think about these things; instead we just keep on muddling through, sometimes with vague feelings of discontent, rather than stop and take stock of what we are doing with our life.

Considering the many hours you spend at work, you may as well invest in half an hour's reflection on its significance for you. When you find that you are unhappy with your job then you have a number of options. You can either begin to consider changing to another position, to another company or to an entirely new profession, or you can create a separate 'second world' in your private life by getting involved in a pastime and thus producing a counterbalance to work.

Financial commitments can make it difficult or even impossible to leave your job and become a sheep farmer, a poet or a ski instructor, just as being a mother of small children is an occupation that you cannot simply throw overboard without considerable damage to yourself and others. It is, however, worth the effort to at least work on improving your position, be it as a parent or a professional person, and there are always ways of rearranging your present situation and making it more satisfactory for yourself.

STEP 3
Assess your present situation concerning your time outside work.

– What do you occupy your free time with?

If you are overworking (see previous chapter) there is no time for leisure activities. This is not a satisfactory state of affairs because it is what you do in your spare time that is what you *want* to do, rather than what you *have* to do. Time away from work is the ideal time to express yourself, be yourself, without any restraints. When I say 'work' I'm talking about an outside job, but I'm also talking about your job as a mother or a housewife. No matter what your job is, make sure you build up something special, something you enjoy. Don't lose sight of your dreams and wishes in the struggle to earn money and bring up the kids. Spending time on cultivating a hobby is just as important as going to work. Getting absorbed in an activity is a way of being in harmony with yourself, and not only will it bring you pleasure, but it will also further your development as a person.

If you can only get involved in your work and neglect your pastime you are putting all your eggs in one basket. You are building up a big stumbling block for when you retire or when the children leave home.

Go through the subsections of Step 1 and start collecting ideas. Do it now while you are reading this chapter. Make a list and you will see that while you are thinking about it, ideas start coming into your mind. Jot down everything, even if it seems ridiculous or unimportant at first, don't edit, don't amend, just get it down on paper as it comes to your head. Spend some time thinking about the various points, go through them in your mind. Can you see yourself engaging in that particular pastime? Which has the most emotional appeal?

STEP 4
Make time for yourself.

This could mean that you need to rearrange your priorities and allocate less time to others and more time to yourself. I know this sounds selfish, but is it really? Isn't it better to be happy and content and give a little less than to be tense and dissatisfied when you are with others? Giving your entire time to others means that you love them very much, but it also means that you don't love yourself enough. If you allow this imbalance to establish itself, you will have to pay the price for it sooner or later, either in form of exhaustion or illness or moodiness.

Reserving your time in the day for yourself helps you take a step back from the rat-race and to recharge your batteries. You are going to be more even-tempered and relaxed for it and in much better shape to work and help others efficiently.

STEP 5
Take reasonable risks.

Sometimes we are forced by life to take risks that we would not normally take. Illness, unemployment, death of a spouse, all of these can push us forward into situations that we would have liked to avoid under normal circumstances. A woman who is left alone with her children after her husband's death sees herself forced to go back to work, although she is worried about having lost her skills and having to struggle to keep up with younger colleagues; in other words, circumstances compel her to expose herself to the risk of failing. When she has finally taken the big step and found herself a job, she goes through a few difficult weeks until she has acclimatised, and soon work becomes a manageable part of her life. When you are made redundant you may have to face the risk of uprooting yourself and relocating where you can get a new job. Once you are established in the new job, you may well find that the new area suits you much better, but without the redundancy you would never have made that move.

Going back to work or changing jobs are major changes which are linked to feelings of big risk, and it usually takes us a long time to make up our minds to take action. However, we seem equally reluctant to take much smaller risks such as trying out unusual foods, speaking to new neighbours or telling someone we like them. The more we cling to old ways the more difficult we find it to cope with sudden changes or with new opportunities.

Why do you find it so difficult to help a new colleague? Is it that you are afraid she might take up too much of your time? Or that she might ask you questions you cannot answer? Or that she might be after your job? In other words, are you taking an unreasonable personal risk by cooperating with her? Only you can assess how big a risk you believe you are taking, but every once in a while it is useful to consciously expand your comfortable boundaries and go just that one step further than you would normally go. It doesn't have to be something wildly daring that you undertake, it could just be something slightly unusual which you would not normally do, such as speaking to the receptionist who you have always overlooked; or taking the bus rather than your car to go to the countryside; or contributing to a conversation when you would normally be silent. Of course you may be less comfortable on the bus, but then it may also give you a different view to see the landscape from the top of a double-decker without having to watch out for the traffic. Of course the receptionist could give you a peculiar look when you stop to chat to her, but then she might turn out to be a nice person. You may be taking certain risks, but at the same time you are likely to gain something from your efforts. It is in your interest to take these small risks because they make life more exciting and more enjoyable. Nothing ventured, nothing gained!

LEARN TO SEE THE SUCCESSFUL OUTCOME

Your expectations reveal a lot about your personality. I'm sure you know someone who will respond to the outline of a new idea by running off a list of reasons why your idea is not going to work. When, as a result, you feel quite deflated and discouraged, he will apologise to you but point out that his objections only show that he is realistic; but as we have seen in Chapter 4, pessimism cannot claim to be the whole truth. Expecting the worst is just as unrealistic as seeing everything through rose-tinted spectacles. Optimism and pessimism are the signposts pointing in opposite directions at a crossroads, and it is your personal choice which direction you want to go. You are as happy as you have made up your mind to be.

Being optimistic is not the same thing as being out of touch with reality; it does not mean that you deny the existence of obstacles, it just means that you expect to master the obstacles. The pessimist will not try anything new if he can help it. He obstructs his own progress by piling up imagined stumbling blocks in his mind until he can't see his aim any more. Pessimism is self-defeating and self-fulfilling, just as optimism is self-promoting and self-fulfilling.

The way you think has a direct influence on how you are feeling and acting. In my book *Positive Thinking*, I have already dealt with this topic in great detail, but I will briefly go over it here because it is of importance when it comes to your personal development.

Let me give you an example. If I put a wooden plank thirty centimetres wide and three metres long on the floor and then asked you to walk across it, you could do that quite easily. But what would happen if I suspended that same plank only two metres above the ground? You begin to think about the distance to the ground, the possibility of falling off, hurting yourself, and you start to tremble a bit. As you are walking across that same plank now, you are less sure-footed, even though the plank is still the same width. Because you are thinking about possible danger your brain sends warning signals to your body and you begin to tense up, and this makes falling off more likely. If I suspended the plank two metres in the air but, with the help of an optical illusion, made it look as though it was on solid ground, you would relax again and walk confidently.

Expecting the successful outcome makes success more likely; expecting problems and occupying your mind with complications produces doubt and trepidation and jeopardises the successful outcome.

Positive or negative expectations can make all the difference when it comes to reaching your goal. They have an influence on your persistence, stamina and also on the success of your venture.

Expectations become reality more easily than we think: our attitudes shape our future.

STEP-BY-STEP GUIDE

STEP 1
Spend time thinking about your aim.

Remember that feeling of being in love, when you can't stop thinking of someone, and every free minute is spent daydreaming about that person? You go around and feel like kissing complete strangers in the street because you are on cloud nine. Just thinking of the other person makes you happy and elated.

Create the same sort of attitude towards you aim. Spend time thinking about it, make it a focal point of your life. It is exciting and fulfilling to strive for new objectives. Get into the swing of positive thinking and of looking forward to working on your aim.

STEP 2
Visualise the successful outcome.

As we have seen in the plank example, indulging in pessimistic thoughts is detrimental to the success of your mission because it allows doubts about your abilities to creep in and shake your confidence.

Visualising means seeing something in your mind's eye and forgetting for a moment where you are. Project your thoughts into the future for just a few minutes and see yourself as having achieved your aim. If you want to learn to swim, see yourself doing several lengths in a pool or swimming in the sea; if your aim is to get promoted, see yourself in a better position, in your own office, working efficiently, being competent and in control; if your aim is to become more self-confident with the opposite sex, see yourself speaking freely and in a relaxed way with someone you like.

When you come across problems on the way to your aim, you will obviously have to deal with them by working out a solution and overcoming them. While you are doing so, however, it can be very useful to visualise the successful outcome, as if you had already overcome the obstacle, to keep your spirits up. When you are embroiled in a complication you can get close to giving up because there doesn't seem to be a way out. Visualisation keeps you going through the difficult stretches, and it may just make the difference between making it or abandoning your project. Remember that just because you cannot think of a solution does not mean that there is no solution.

By tackling a new project, you introduce variety and richness into your life, and if you go for it, go for it one hundred percent. Don't capitulate in the face of problems. Always remember your aim. The more clearly you keep it in your mind, the more positive you will feel and the more likely it is that you will succeed.

VISUALISATION EXERCISE

To get the maximum effect from visualisation, sit down comfortably and close your eyes. Begin to listen to your breathing for a moment to help you focus your mind onto yourself. Then imagine yourself in a particualr situation or imagine watching a film about yourself in that situation: feel it, see it, try to be there.

Let me give you a few examples. Let us assume you are aiming for a little repair business that you run from home.

See yourself looking at a paper with your advertisement in it . . . see yourself answering the phone and imagine yourself dealing with enquiries . . . fixing appointments with prospective customers . . . leaving the house with your tool kit . . . carrying out the repair at the customer's place . . . collecting the fee . . . feeling good about it.

Or learning to swim:

See or feel yourself getting into the water, at the end where you still have ground under your feet . . . feel the water up to your waist . . . feel how you let yourself gently drift forward into the swimming position . . . floating . . . as you calmly begin to move your arms and legs . . . synchronising your motions . . . floating comfortably . . . breathing easily . . . calm and relaxed and concentrated on what you are doing . . . doing stroke after stroke . . . until you are at the other end of the pool . . . feeling good.

Or finally redecorating your living room:

See yourself getting all the tools out, ladder, rolls of wallpaper, paste brush etc. . . . see the living room ready, prepared to start the job . . . carpet and furniture covered up . . . see yourself removing the old wallpaper easily . . . hanging the new one . . . doing the last strip . . . taking all the covers off . . . putting things back into place in the room . . . and see the new image of the room . . . and feel good about it.

Visualisation is not only useful to see you through difficult patches, it is also a great help when you cannot get motivated to start a job. Visualise regularly, preferably several times a day, and in the end you won't be able to stop yourself from tackling the task!

LEARN TO STOP PUTTING YOURSELF DOWN

Hiding your light under a bushel is as much a male issue as a female one; the only difference is that women are more obviously self-depreciating whereas men tend to mask it more, camouflaging insecurity with tough talk or behaviour. In my practice I see just as many men as women putting themselves down, hating themselves for their weaknesses, their inability to communicate, their negative feelings towards themselves and others. Taking these clients through analysis I find the same pattern over and over again: a childhood where the parents were emotionally abusive or simply didn't care for the child. The social background can be anything from working class to aristocracy: money does not make an iota of difference. If a child is unloved it won't know how to love itself. If there is no security and emotional reliability, the child cannot grow into a stable adult. No matter how many toys you give that child, it will not be able to like itself because to a child's mind, a lack of care and attention can only mean one thing: it doesn't deserve the parents' love because it is in some way deficient. This is how an inferiority complex comes about.

One of our basic human needs is to be recognised by

others as a worthy person. We want to be seen as interesting and special, we want other people to think of us as
knowledgeable and competent – and to like us as a consequence. It is very important for us to feel accepted by
others; after all we share our world with lots of other
people, be they family, friends, neighbours or colleagues
at work, and our personal growth is determined by how
successfully we participate in our social environment.

On the other hand, there is the notion of modesty with
all its implications. We are told that it is 'not nice' to talk
about our own achievements because that would be boast-
ing; we should not be too concerned about our looks
because that would be vain. Instead, we are advised to be
modest and hide our achievements so they do not attract
public attention. This is why some women can go to great
lengths dressing up for a special occasion, taking a lot of
care in choosing an elegant outfit, carefully putting on
make-up, getting their hair just right, selecting matching
accessories, only to reply, 'Oh this old thing! I've had it for
years!' when someone pays them a compliment.

A similar thing can happen in the work environment.
You are slaving away at a project, writing up the results in
a report in endless hours of overtime and then hand the
result to your boss who publishes the findings under his
name. This should be fine by you because, under the laws
of self-denial, you are supposed to be content with having
contributed to the final project. You know all that and
you should be content with that knowledge – no need to
publicise your contribution really, because that would be
drawing attention to yourself unnecessarily. . .

Unfortunately this only works in theory. As you are still
a human being who needs recognition, your feelings begin
to rebel at this point. Why should your boss get all the
credit when you have done practically all the work? Why
don't you get a higher salary if your work is good enough
to pass as your boss's? But no, you quickly suppress these
thoughts, they are not the thoughts of a nice person. And
you don't want to be considered big-headed by pushing
yourself into the limelight like that! Better to forget your
feelings and start on the next project. . .

The only problem is that your feelings of having been

treated unfairly will not yield just like that, no matter how much you fight them on a conscious level. The idea of self-denial is all well and good as long as the matter isn't important to you. But once you put a lot of energy into something, it is only natural that you want your efforts recognised, and this has nothing to do with being immodest.

Not taking credit where it is due is a way of putting yourself down. You may think that it is your boss's fault because he or she should really be acknowledging your contribution voluntarily. This is quite true; but it is also your own fault for letting your boss get away with it. You may not be able to convince him or her to publicly announce your part in the project, but the least you can do for your self-esteem is to address the matter the next time you are speaking to your boss ('Were you happy with the report I wrote for you? Did everything go well at the presentation?'). This will bring the fact to your boss's attention that *you* concocted this fabulous piece of work.

When you stop to think for a moment who benefits from your modesty, you will find that it is never you (that is unless you get a kick out of being the underdog). Your modesty keeps your salary down, hinders your professional progress and upsets your emotional balance. Conversely, your modesty helps your boss gain prestige without having to work for it.

If you have talents you owe it to yourself to make the most of them, and that means not just putting in the work but also reaping the rewards. It is practically impossible to remain motivated when there is no return awaiting you at the end. The concept of modesty is advantageous only to the person who suggests it to you. The dimmer you switch your light, the brighter theirs will shine.

Being inappropriately modest is a passive way of putting yourself down. For one reason or another you feel inhibited about acknowledging your own achievements and therefore you won't ensure that they are rewarded.

Another way of putting yourself down is that of speaking in a disparaging manner of yourself and your abilities by constantly criticising yourself and automatically assuming responsibility for everything that goes wrong in your social environment. People who apologise all the time belong to that category. It is as if they feel guilty about this inadequacy and prefer to point it out themselves rather than wait until someone else does it. Better to humiliate yourself than to be humiliated by another person. The effect is, of course, that as the person starts denigrating himself, his friends feel obliged to contradict him and all the others start using him. And although the self-accuser does not trust his friends' assurances (because he doesn't trust anybody, least of all himself), he still feels good about the moral support he is getting. However, the moral support can only ever be a prop – it cannot make up for a lack of confidence and self-esteem. Even if you encourage someone with a negative attitude about themselves, you can only redress the emotional balance momentarily; the underlying problem is still the same. So what can you do?

Self-accusation is by no means a sure way of averting criticism. When things go wrong, it is usually the weakest person in the set-up who will be given the blame, and if you are someone who apologises a lot you are predestined to become the scapegoat, *whether it was your fault or not*. You are behaving like the underdog, so you get treated as one.

STEP-BY-STEP GUIDE

STEP 1
Assess your self-image.

Imagine you could look at youself from the outside, as if you were your own best friend, and imagine someone asked that friend to describe you. How do you think that friend would assess you? Write down a little report. Having it black on white is going to make it clearer and more definite in your mind.

The description would, of course, be a benevolent one, because it is made by someone who likes you. Try to see yourself through someone else's eyes and then decide what you would say about your person and your achievements. Should this be too abstract for you, ask a few friends how they would describe you to someone else.

The reason why your self-assessment should be made by a sympathetic person is that you are already good at putting yourself down, but not so good at looking at your positive points. However, no-one in this world has only bad points, not even you, so you are being unrealistic by leaving your negative attitude unchallenged.

Step 2
Act out your good points.

Once you have at least three positive traits of character together, begin to act as if they were true, even if you don't believe that they are. If your friends have described you as generous, watch out for any signs in your behaviour that indicate that your friends are right. If you have described yourself as a problem-solver, think back to any events in the past where you successfully tackled problems, either your own or other people's. What evidence is there to corroborate your positive assessment? For a couple of weeks, take any opportunity to get to work on difficult situations and set out to prove that you can do what others think you can do. As you achieve your first successes, you are making a positive self-image become reality. By being optimistic you create a saintly (as opposed to a vicious) circle: you make out something positive about yourself is true and in the end it becomes true.

Step 3
Learn to accept praise.

Not accepting compliments and praise is the display of a false sense of modesty. You pretend that you don't deserve the applause when you have just worked your guts out to get it. Why is it so difficult for some people to acknowledge praise graciously? Our rules of etiquette seem to emphasise the giving more than the taking. We are taught how to give presents, how to hold the door open for someone else, how to offer an elderly person a seat on the tube, but we do not hear much about how to accept all this with pleasure. Some people are positively embarrassed when you remark admiringly on their achievements, some even get cross at you for mentioning it when you would expect them to be delighted at the fact that you have openly acknowledged their success.

Praise is sometimes confused with flattery. If your self-confidence is low you tend to suspect others of dishonesty. As you cannot see yourself in a positive light, you cannot give others credit for being genuinely friendly, therefore you must necessarily assume that they are untruthful with you. It is a fact that there are people who will flatter you. to manipulate you, but it is also a fact that others are truly pleased for you and want to wish you well. Your overall assessment of that person will have to determine whether you can take the compliment seriously or not.

If you dismiss *all* praise as flattery this is an indication that you are too pessimistic about yourself and others. Go through Step 1 again. There is less harm in accepting too many compliments than in accepting too few, compliments are like presents, and they should be received as such: happily. After all, you don't go red with embarrassment when you open a Christmas present, so why do it when someone gives you a verbal present?

Smile, show that you are happy about it! Don't pretend you don't like it, and don't insult the other person by making out that they are lying to you. There is nothing so discouraging as a gloomy or vexed face when you have just said something nice to a person. The more graciously you can accept, the more likely it is that the other person will openly give you credit for your accomplishments next time around. We all need to be admired and appreciated every once in a while. It is good for body and soul, so let's encourage it!

STEP 4
Be economical with apologies.

You are flattering yourself when you think everything is your fault. You forget that there are other people about and that they exert an influence on daily events just as much as you do. This doesn't mean that you never make mistakes; it only means that you should check out a situation carefully before apologising.

If something goes wrong, speak about it. When a friend

starts treating you in an unfriendly way, ask for an explanation. Don't start apologising for wrongs you imagine you have done when you don't really understand what is going on. Once you have clarified what has led up to the negative vibes you are receiving there is always time to apologise. An apology is useful only when it is followed by a plan of how to avoid the mistake from occurring a second time; otherwise it is like stealing sweets from a shop, going to confession and getting absolution, and then going back again and stuffing your pockets with more sweets in the next shop. No problem, because you can always go to confession the next day. . .

If you apologise, take it seriously and see to it that a similar thing doesn't happen again. An apology is a stepping stone in a learning process that enables people to deal with conflicts in a dignified manner. On their own, apologies are useless. They always have to be preceded by clarification of the situation and followed by active solutions. Any apology is only as good as the action you take to prevent the mistake from occurring again.

Step 5
Be nice to yourself.

Putting someone else down is a humiliating thing to do. If you see a big bossy person harshly criticising someone else, you would not like the bossy person very much – and yet you behave just like a bully towards yourself. You find fault with yourself, nothing you do counts in your favour and you won't allow any achievements to heighten your spirits. Instead, you minimise your successes ('It was just a fluke') or you make out that it could only happen because the time was right or because someone helped you. You may even regret that this success happened because now the contrast will be even more pronounced and you will feel even more miserable when you are not successful next time; or when things go wrong next time you will feel even less capable because you cannot repeat that success.

Having success is not necessarily coupled with liking yourself. Lots of people in high positions who have achieved a great deal in their professions are highly critical of themselves and very unsure of their person. This seems peculiar in the face of the position and status they have reached in life, but it shows that success is relative and depends on how you look at life. Unless you accept and like yourself, all your achievements, good looks and high income will mean nothing. They will not count as long as you cannot allow yourself to feel that you deserve them. Look at the tragic lives of so many film stars. How could they kill themselves? They were so beautiful and so immensely successful, and yet they were hooked on pills and alcohol. If you don't like yourself, the easiest option is to make yourself forget that you exist, and any addictions, be they to food, drugs, alcohol or pills, have that emotional element of self-hate in them. You consider yourself trash, therefore you treat yourself like trash.

Needless to say that this is a self-destructive attitude. As long as you don't like yourself you cannot love anyone else. As long as you are not at home within yourself, you cannot be at home anywhere, no matter where you go. Not liking yourself means sticking knives into your ego every day of the week and not giving yourself a break unless someone you consider to be higher ranking than yourself allows you to do so by giving you praise. And although you don't trust others, you are entirely dependent on their good opinion of you because that is the only break you get from disliking yourself. You resent other people for holding the key to your self-esteem, and at the same time their praise is vital to your emotional survival.

Self-hate can go back to a variety of causes, but generally it can be said that disliking yourself is a reflection of someone else, usually a parent, having disliked you to start off with. As you develop your self-image in your formative years, much will depend on how others react to you. If people who are close to you reject you or ignore you constantly you read this as an interpretation of your person: you are disliked because you are unlovable.

There is no need, however, to carry on in this way, and indeed you shouldn't put up with it. You cannot thrive when you are bogged down by emotional afflictions that are rooted in the past.

There are various ways of learning to treat yourself

better. It is certainly helpful if you can trace back where your lack of self-esteem stems from. It may be due to the way you were brought up, or to bullying at school, or to a particular incident in your life where you feel you failed (see also Chapter 15). Often, one mistake can have such an impact that it appears to alter one's entire life. We cannot forgive ourselves for a weakness or a blunder or a failure and we carry around a millstone of guilt, even though the original incident has long since gone. Being aware of the origin is often enough to turn around your negative self-assessment, but should you feel unable to extricate yourself from past trauma you may want to consider seeking professional psychological help.

Being nice to yourself means not being overcritical, not pushing yourself unreasonably hard, going easy on your body by not overloading it with too much food or alcohol, and generally treating yourself with respect, just as you would treat someone else who is precious to you.

No matter what you do with your life, it is essential to bring your plans and actions into harmony with yourself and your own needs. If you keep ignoring your own wishes you are upsetting your inner balance and treating yourself like a second-class citizen, and your development will be hampered. Being in harmony with yourself is the prerequisite for personal growth because it gives you a firm basis from which you can operate.

LEARN TO STOP GENERALISING

When you cannot cope with everyday life, you start generalising. When outside pressure becomes unbearable, you start generalising and seeking for the culprit outside. You allocate the fault to someone else or to an institution: it is the government, the state of our democracy or the 'system' which does not allow you to express yourself/be more relaxed/get a better job. This is a convenient way of looking at life, albeit highly unproductive. As long as you can find someone else to pass the buck to, you needn't do anything yourself. You withdraw to your ivory tower and contemplate the world from your unworldly position, philosophising on theoretical issues.

It is of course true that institutions and their bureaucracies do not always work to our advantage and that we are living in a male-dominated world, and there may well be cause for complaint. As mentioned in Chapter 1, we are limited in our activities by the society we live in, by its rules and regulations, but there is still enough room for us to manœuvre reasonably freely.

STEP-BY-STEP GUIDE

STEP 1
Trace your generalisations back to the actual problem.

Let me give you an example. I had a client who kept saying that society was making people ill and that he felt very depressed about this. He spent considerable time speaking about how we lived in an uncaring society and how this society turned one person against the other. He himself, however, considered himself a caring person, one of the few. When I enquired into the background of this sudden depression, it turned out that he had had a row with his friend, an emotionally unstable girl. During that quarrel, she had abused him and called him names. He didn't dare shout back at her although he was angry at the unjust accusations and the bad language she used; rather than stand up for himself he retreated into the excuse that she was ill and he was caring and understanding, as opposed to the rest of the world who had made his girlfriend into an emotional wreck. His great fear of arguments and his lack of self-respect prevented him from venting his anger, but like the steam of a boiling kettle, the emotion had to go somewhere. As it wasn't allowed to be turned outside, it got bottled up inside which resulted in the depression.

He had used the shortcomings of society to mask his inability to stop his girlfriend from verbally abusing him. Once he recognised his avoidance tactics and started working on the actual self-confidence problem, he began to feel more in control and was able to prevent rows from escalating to their former pitch; in fact he reported that once he had shown his discontent with her behaviour, she treated him more kindly and the relationship became happier altogether.

STEP 2
Tackle the actual problem.

When generalisations are used as excuses, they usually camouflage a fear that seems invincible. The fear, however, is often worse than the object or situation it is attached to. How often have we been worried about an event and then found that it turned out to be quite harmless and not at all as we expected! All the horror pictures you built up in your mind dissolved into thin air as you actually faced the situation.

You may find it impossible to speak your mind at work for fear of losing your job. When you finally do, not only do you find that you don't lose your job, but you actually get what you want.

STEP 3
Take responsibility for yourself.

When you blame the 'system' for the fact that you cannot achieve what you would like to achieve, you are saying that you are helpless and incapable of independent action. As a therapist I am aware that some people genuinely feel out of control of their life, in which case it is necessary to seek professional help. But most of us know full well that we could be doing more to further our cause if only we made the effort, and that is where our accountability lies. Once we can overcome our apathy and stop blaming others for our own shortcomings we are beginning to take control and direct our own play. If we allow others to write our scripts we abdicate responsibility and we will be treated accordingly. It may sound like the easy way out but it is certainly not the best way. As you are the only person who truly understands your own needs (provided you have taken the time to find out what they are), it is unlikely that others will be able to act in your best interest. Taking responsibility for yourself means that you need to stand up and be counted by speaking about your needs, by taking appropriate action to bring you closer to your aims and by accepting the fact that you might sometimes make mistakes in the process.

At no time have social circumstances been perfect, and yet there have always been people who succeeded, no matter what problems they came up against, and other people who failed, no matter what opportunities came their way. It is up to you which group you want to belong to.

We do have a say in the direction our life takes, and even though we may be confused as to where to go, we can always buy a map and inform ourselves about the possible roads we can take. There is no right or wrong way to go, there is only *your* way.

STEP 4
Establish your values.

A teacher of mine used to lament how the world had changed for the worse since he was a child, that people nowadays didn't have ideals and that all the old values had been abolished without being replaced by new ones. At the time, I remember nodding my head and feeling sad at the thought that the world was rapidly going downhill, just hoping that I would be able to get off before it hit rock-bottom.

Now as I think back to my teacher's discourse, I feel quite differently about the issues he raised. What made him come to the conclusion that the old values had been invalidated, and what are these 'values' anyway? It sounded as though he meant qualities like honesty, decency and reliability. How can you abolish them? Do you declare them null and void by public decree? Or do people simply forget that they exist and consequently act in a dishonest, careless and inconsiderate way?

I believe that the old values are still around, alive and kicking, and very much in demand. It may well be that our moral code and social etiquette has become more liberal and that this makes people less restricted in what they can openly speak about. This may be uncomfortable for some who wish old taboos such as incest, rape or homosexuality were not raised in public, but at the same time it also helps to protect those who have been victims of abuse and to broaden general attitudes.

In order to establish which values you have, think about the qualities you expect in a good friend; these can be loyalty, commitment, honesty, support and so on. You can even rank these qualities according to your personal preference, and as you do so, these values become quite tangible. They become real because you can apply them to particular situations. You can tell honesty because you have experienced dishonesty; you recognise commitment because you have met with neglect or disinterest.

Your values will depend on the situations and problems you have encountered in your life, so values cannot be generalised but need to be assessed in a personal light. Your values are directly linked to your attitudes and your way of thinking and as such they are an expression of you as a person. In the process of getting to know yourself you will also have to establish at one point what your values are. Working on achieving for yourself the qualities you seek in others may well be one of your aims of personal development.

LEARN TO STOP WANTING TO PLEASE

Trying to please other people is a full-time occupation which offers low returns and a minimal success rate for a maximum of input; in other words it is not worth your while if you value your emotional well-being. Also, it just doesn't work, not for you nor for anyone else involved. The reason why it doesn't work is because when you are endlessly trying to please others you are not being yourself.

STEP-BY-STEP GUIDE

STEP 1
Be yourself.

This sounds easy but is probably the most difficult thing. The moment you ask someone to act naturally they become self-conscious and can't be natural any more. How do you go about being yourself? This question already shows up the underlying contradiction of engineering your own behaviour on the one hand and being as you are, without frills, on the other. There is nothing you can do to be yourself because as soon as you do something, you are manipulating yourself.

Being natural means concentrating on what you are doing rather than concentrating on yourself. When you are having a conversation with a friend, you are natural when you are wrapped up in what your friend is saying, *not* when you wonder whether you should touch up your make-up or whether you should sit on the other side of him because that brings out your profile better. Being yourself means forgetting about yourself, not worrying about what others think, nor worrying about what you look like or sound like. This, of course, is like telling someone not to think of a pink elephant: the first image that pops into your mind, even if you have never thought of one before in your life, is a pink elephant.

The answer is to focus your mind on what you are doing. Concentrate with all your senses on the activity you are involved in, take an interest in what you are working on and get absorbed in it. Pay attention to detail. If you are digging up the garden, look at the colour of the earth, the shape and number of stones in it, the creatures that live in it. Be aware of the colour of the sky, the breeze, the feel of the spade as it digs into the ground. When you are speaking to a colleague at work, observe her facial expression, her gestures, pay attention to what she is saying and how she is saying it. Focusing on a matter or on another person automatically takes your attention away from yourself. Not only does that make you less self-conscious, it also gets you better results in what you are doing.

For some people it is difficult to 'let go' and really take

an interest in what they are doing because they constantly observe themselves, judging themselves as if standing next to themselves, a bit like the washing powder advertisement on television where the housewife's conscience suddenly emerges out of her in the shape of a second person, reprimanding her for not having got her laundry perfectly clean.

This fault-seeking attitude towards yourself is caused by previous experiences where you were repeatedly criticised by someone else. This may go back to your childhood or it could be rooted in the more recent past. Being judged harshly erodes your self-confidence and instils doubts in you as to whether you are doing things right, and in the end you internalise the criticism which then takes the form of a guilty conscience. Even though the person who originally censured you is no longer around, your conscience does his job for him: you criticise yourself. In other words, you cannot allow yourself to divert your attention away from your person and get on with what you really want to do.

It is important to be yourself because that is the most harmonious way to live. Blaming and criticising yourself constantly wastes a lot of energy, as does acting against your own interests by trying to please others all the time. When it comes to the crunch you need to be able to determine what it is *you* want, or you will find yourself at the end of your days having lived someone else's life and not your own.

STEP 2
Allow others to be as they are.

A guaranteed recipe for disaster is to try to change others. It is an illusion to think that you can transform your partner's behaviour once you are married; many couples have found that out to their detriment. The only person who can change your partner is your partner him- or herself, and this will happen either because your partner wants to change or because you change your behaviour towards your partner.

In order to change you have to be willing to change, you have to want to gain insight into your person, and neither of this can be achieved by outside pressure. It is a voluntary act to work on yourself. In my hypnotherapy practice I see a great number of clients with emotional problems, and every once in a while I get phonecalls from people who ask for a brochure to be sent to a friend or relative of theirs 'because they could do with some psychotherapy'. I always explain to those callers that there is little point in me sending out information about my practice to a person who does not want treatment. Instead, I suggest they speak to their friend and pass on my telephone number so that when they are ready they can ring me themselves. I will also not accept someone for treatment when I find out during the introductory consultation that they were pressurised into it by a relative and that they themselves didn't really want to come.

You should not give in to the misconception that you can make people change their habits or attitudes or behaviours. But allowing others to be as they are does not mean that you have to take whatever they dish out. When a man gets drunk every night and goes home and beats up his wife and children, I'm all for the woman moving out *because she won't be able to change his behaviour*. When a woman deceives her husband again and again with other men, he will either have to grin and bear it or get out of the relationship *because he cannot change her*.

Ideally we will pick our friends and lovers from a category of people that makes us feel at ease. If it is a strain to keep the relationship going, if we have to make strenuous efforts to please the other person, we are not well suited to one another.

STEP 3
What is the price you are paying for pleasing?

Your decisions should be made because of what *you* think is best, not because of what you think others expect of you. If someone asks you for a favour, your consent should not be an automatic mechanism within you that starts operating immediately when someone makes a request. Think about it: do you really want to do what is being asked of you? Do you have to put yourself out to an unreasonable extent in order to help, and if so, do you really want to? Do you want to help that particular person?

A client of mine, let us call her Doris, felt very dissatisfied with her life and herself because she could not cope with her mother. The old lady was ill with an injury on her leg which confined her to bed in the rest home where she was living.

The rest home was a two hour bus ride from Doris's home. As Doris was a single mother and also keeping down a full-time job, it took a lot of organising on her part to go down to the home and visit her mother once a week. Her mother was quite a difficult person, domineering and querulous at the best of times, and her illness hadn't helped to improve her moods. Doris dreaded the weekly visits. Although she went to the trouble of always taking a little present, her mother would rarely show any signs of enthusiasm about her visits. After only about ten minutes her mother would ostentatiously close her eyes, turn away from Doris and ask her to go because she was tired. Initially, Doris got very concerned about her mother's weak state until she heard from one of the nurses that her mother was sitting up in bed all day and all evening throughout the rest of the week without as much as taking a nap after lunch.

Doris began to feel annoyed but at the same time help-less. Her mother didn't have many friends, her husband had died a long time ago and Doris's brother lived in a remote part of the country, so Doris was the only relative close at hand and she felt it was her duty to see her mother regularly. But with every visit and every unfriendly brush-off she felt less and less like going, and the duty became a chore. She felt she had to go because she couldn't live with her guilty conscience if she didn't. She also felt she had to be patient and friendly with her mother because she was old and not very well. However, she admitted to me that she didn't like being treated rudely for all her troubles.

Doris was a gentle and friendly lady who would always seek fault with herself before pointing the finger at anyone else, and she had great doubts about the concept of stand-ing up for herself, let alone defending herself against her mother's abrupt manners. She was afraid of being too sharp with a defenceless person, but at the same time her feelings were telling her clearly that she bitterly resented being pushed around like that. We decided therefore that it would be worth taking the risk of finding out what would happen if Doris changed to a firmer attitude towards her mother. It took her a few more visits until she managed to do so, but then she did it very well, and with surprising results.

Once again, her mother had asked her to leave after a short while. Rather than meekly (but angrily) leaving the room, Doris stated that she had no intention of leaving after only fifteen minutes when she had been on the bus for two hours, and that if her mother didn't try to be a bit nicer she would not come to see her for a while. The mother turned around to Doris, took her hand and for the first time in her life thanked her daughter for looking after her and told her that she loved her. The following visits went exceptionally well, with the mother being polite and enquiring about her daughter's work, and although the mother would occasionally slip back into her old ways, Doris was able to stand her ground and the visits became much more enjoyable to both of them.

After standing up for herself for the first time, Doris reported that it had been a revelation to her that she had achieved more by being herself than she had all those years by trying to please her mother.

STEP 4
Please yourself before you please others.

I would like to emphasise that being yourself does not mean being rude or inconsiderate; it just means living in harmony with your own feelings. You will still have to negotiate with others for what you want, but by being yourself you become an equal partner in the negotiating process. It is irresponsible to let anger build up to an extent where the slightest incident will trigger an explosion. Before you can please others, you need to learn how to please yourself; only then will you be able to give freely to others, and to give because you want to give, and not out of duty or because you think the other person expects it. It is better to give less and give it happily than to give a lot and do it grudgingly.

It is important to learn to say no when you don't want to do something. If you say 'yes' and feel 'no', you are creating a conflict which leads to stress, and the more often you create this imbalance within yourself, the less you feel in control of yourself and your life.

There are various ways of expressing yourself. Some people find it easier than others to speak in a straightforward manner about what they want and don't want, and there is no one way that is the right way of doing it. You can speak in a quiet voice and still be assertive. It is *what* you say that is important for your emotional balance, and it is *how* you say it that will determine how well you are doing in your negotiations with others. Being hysterical or aggressive detracts from your credibility, and it also makes other people feel cornered, and although they may do what you want them to, they do it under duress, and this is not a good form of cooperation.

What counts is that your actions are in harmony with your feelings, and you will end up being a freer and happier person for it. If you are trying to please others all the time, you are neglecting yourself. Don't put others on a pedestal, they are only human, just like you. Don't forget: the happier you are, the happier you can make others!

LEARN TO OVERCOME APATHY

Please do not confuse apathy with relaxation – they are two fundamentally different things, although they may look the same from the outside. When you are relaxed, your body and mind work in harmony together, whereas in the case of apathy, your body may be motionless, but your mind is not at all at peace. Apathy is unhappy listlessness, where nothing appeals anymore, where life has lost its taste, shape and colour and where nothing has meaning for you. Most of us have encountered a mild variant of this feeling at one time or another: we would like to shape up but we cannot get motivated to go to a gym; we have been working

on a project for a long time and now we have lost interest
and don't want to tackle it any longer; we are undergoing
an emotionally stressful situation which seems to suck out
all our life energy. Other reasons may be that we are overworked or seriously underworked or that we feel defeated
by a stroke of bad luck and have switched into passive
mode as a consequence. Emotional numbness can also be
a side-effect of an underlying depression which dates back
to unresolved conflicts in the past that have been repressed
and are no longer consciously remembered.

Overcoming listlessness is particularly difficult because
you have to get motivated in order to want to beat your
lack of motivation; the tool and the problem are one and
the same thing. However, as long as there is a fragment of
motivation left, you can build on that and gradually extend
it until you are satisfied with your degree of activeness.

To begin with, it is important to clarify the facts.

STEP-BY-STEP GUIDE

STEP 1

Are you overworked or underworked?

The way you tackle your listlessness will depend on a variety
of aspects. In order to find out what the best angle of attack
is you will have to determine whether your apathy is due to
work overload or the absence of challenges or demands in
your life. The latter can occur when you get into a routine
where you become mentally and physically lazy because you
consciously or subconsciously avoid stimuli. This can happen
as a consequence of having lost or given up your job, for
example, or after a long illness. The longer you avoid doing
new things and tackling fresh challenges, the more scared
you are of eventually embarking on a new enterprise. The
longer you have been out of work, the more doubts you
accumulate as to whether you will be able to deal with the
demands of the workplace; the longer you have been physically unwell the greater your doubts about your stamina and
your capability to see a new thing through. In these situations
it seems safer to remain where you are than to venture out

into the world and possibly fail. We have got to exercise our initiative regularly or we lose it eventually.

When you are overworked, your apathy is a symptom of the stress you are under: because you do not have time to catch your breath, you automatically cut out any activities that do not appear to be strictly necessary, and very often, those are activities that concern your private interests. You feel you *should* pursue a hobby, but after a hard day's work you simply cannot muster the strength to initiate any action; instead, you flop in front of the TV, eat a meal and drop into bed.

In a case like that, the apathy has to be tackled via the work overload. There is no point in deciding to 'pull yourself together' and push yourself even harder to do an evening class on top of everything else. This would only mean over- loading your system even further. You will have to sort out your work situation, and when I say 'work' I mean anything from being a housewife and mother to being an executive for a multinational concern. When you find that your work is ruling you rather than you ruling your work, it is time to step in and take measures to get the situation under control again (see also p. 79 'Learn how to do nothing').

If, on the other hand, you are underworked, you need to approach apathy in a different manner. I have a friend in the States, a lady of 35 with a husband and a teenage daughter and a house with swimming pool on the outskirts of Pitts- burgh. She works two half-days a week as a dental nurse, has a fully equipped kitchen and serves mainly pre-cooked meals. She enjoys sitting by her swimming pool, reading books and sipping drinks. Disaster strikes, however, when washday comes. My friend dislikes washdays more than anything else in the world, except perhaps ironing. She will spend two whole days getting ready for the big event, roaming the house, sighing heavily and moaning at the injustice of fate, until she finally gathers the clothes from the laundry basket, takes them downstairs and stuffs them in the washing machine. Together with sorting out the white laundry from the coloured and putting washing powder into the machine, the whole procedure takes about ten minutes; the run-up to it, however, is something else and needs to be seen to be believed.

When you have been out of your active mode for a while, listlessness becomes something of a bad habit and you need to learn how to expose yourself gradually to more stress again (see Step 3). While you are doing that you may occasionally come to a point where you ask yourself, 'Why am I doing this to myself?' and feel tired and exhausted about your new efforts which may not always turn out as successfully as you would wish them to. But then you were not particularly content being listless, so at least now you are beginning to achieve something, and once you are back into the swing of being more active, you will begin to enjoy your activities more and become more successful. It is really only a matter of getting over the first few weeks, and once you have passed that period of time you will feel a lot better for having made the effort.

STEP 2
How serious is your apathy?

a) I have always been a lazy person. I enjoy sitting around doing nothing.

b) I cannot face having to do chores around the house, such as ironing, gardening, doing repairs etc.

c) I lost my job some time ago and now I am so used to not working that I have lost all motivation to look for a new job.

d) I've nearly completed my degree course, and now I find I cannot motivate myself to work for the exam.

e) I cannot be bothered to look after myself (for example losing weight, shaping up, getting a decent haircut, putting on nicer clothes) even though I would like to look and feel better.

f) I have been unable to take any interest in life since my husband died/my girlfriend left me.

g) I cannot leave the house because I feel anxious about open spaces. I am scared of everything and anything.

Comments:

a) Great! If sitting around doing nothing has entertainment value for you, then you should go on enjoying it. You don't have a problem – as long as you don't mind other people finding you a bit boring.

b) Understandable. It is a commonplace phenomenon that, as soon as an unpleasant task lurks, your energy level drops to zero. See Step 3 for suggestions.

c) and d) Understandable. Slightly more far-reaching consequences than b) because you have more to lose if you don't get to grips with the drop in your energy level.

e) Action required. What happened to your self-esteem? This needs investigating. See Step 3 and also chapter 15.

f) Serious. You will need a lot of help from friends or possibly professional help if you feel things are getting out of hand.

g) Serious. Seek professional psychological help. See also chapter 15.

Step 3
Make a minimal commitment and tell everyone about it.

Just as with many other aspects of personal development, the most constructive approach is to pick a target and dissect the path to your aim into manageable small steps. It is a bit like training a muscle that you haven't used for a long time: you cannot put full strain on it straight away. Instead, you have got to warm it up slowly, and gradually it will be able to take a higher load.

For the hardened lethargic, it can already be an insurmountable task to choose an aim. When you have not taken much interest in what is going on around you, you may feel very unsure about what sort of target to strive for. In that case it may be easiest to concentrate initially on things that need to be done anyway, rather than on a new hobby for example.

Let us look at an example. Say you need to write a letter of complaint to the supplier of your three-piece-suite because you received one chair with a soiled armrest.

Task	Time spent doing task
a) Find the supplier's address and/or delivery note.	1 – 10 minutes
b) Make notes of the facts: What was delivered, when it was delivered and what is wrong with it. Jot down what you want done about the fault (replacement/money back/cleaning costs reimbursed).	1 – 5 minutes
c) Make your notes into whole sentences.	10 minutes
d) Write or type the final letter.	10 – 15 minutes
e) Post the letter on your way to work/to the shops.	

This list may look very pedantic and even faintly ridiculous to you, seeing all these little steps and the approximate time it takes to do them, but there is a reason why I have broken the task down in this manner. When you add up the maximum time it takes to complete the letter, you will see that it comes to 40 minutes. This is allocating time for searching for the delivery note and inadequate typing skills that hold you up. Once you get the hang of it, the same task can be done in about half that time. An average of half an hour to get a task out of the way is really not that bad, is it? Even if you are working during the week, you could easily slot in this activity somewhere during the weekend, and you would still have lots of time to do other things.

We often overestimate the time it takes us to get something done, just because we don't like starting on the task that lies ahead, and when we finally get around to it, we are surprised at how quickly it is completed.

It can be useful if you tell others of your decision to start on a project and ask them to help you by reminding you on a day of your choice. Once you have announced publicly that you are going to do something it is just that little bit harder to abandon the idea.

When your aim is more complex, you may have to allow for several days to accomplish it, but the procedure remains the same. Remember that *any* new step you take is progress and is leading in the right direction, namely out of apathy.

Talking to other people about your plans can also have the added benefit that you may find someone who wants to share your new activity. It can often be easier to see something through to the end if you are joined by another person. Targets like losing weight or going to exercise or evening classes can be easier to reach if you can encourage one another and help each other through rough patches like, for example, flagging enthusiasm.

STEP 4
Don't try to be perfect.

As you are making your first attempts to escape the lethargy trap, don't expect flawless results. If you feel that your letter of complaint could be worded better but you cannot think how to put it any more elegantly, send it anyway. As long as it has all the facts in it, the supplier will know what you mean. The choice is not whether you should send a well-written letter or a poorly-composed one, the choice is whether you should send a letter or not. Once you are in more active mode you can start working on the quality of what you are producing, but until then the main point is to just do it, no matter how well or how badly. You wouldn't dream of sending a six-year-old straight to college – that is only common sense – so be just as sensible when it comes to what you expect of yourself. Get on with the task in hand, but be lenient. You are bound to get better as you go along.

15. IF ALL ELSE FAILS

PROVIDED you are emotionally reasonably balanced, this book can be of great help to you in that it will give you an impetus to try out new things and live your life to the full.

Fulfilling your potential can, however, be blocked by traumatic events that happened to you in the past, and dissolving them may be outside your control. You will have noticed that I mention in several chapters of the book that professional help may be required if you feel unable to overcome particular problems on your own.

As it is difficult to say what state of mind the term 'emotionally reasonably balanced' defines, you may find it easier to think in terms of freedom of action. If you feel that you are unable to do things you would like to do (such as communicating with others; using lifts; being relaxed; enjoying sex) or that you are unable to stop yourself from doing things you would rather not do (such as losing your temper frequently; nailbiting; chain smoking; comfort eating), then you can be sure that there is a more deep-rooted cause at the bottom of your problem.

Other symptoms that indicate an emotional imbalance are bedwetting, some cases of asthma, migraine and PMT, impotence, anorexia nervosa, and bulimia to name but a few.

I always check with prospective clients whether they suffer from any phobias, compulsions or obsessions, because these also indicate a psychological blockage. Phobias are fears of harmless objects and situations. The most common phobias are claustrophobia (fear of enclosed spaces such as lifts) and agoraphobia (fear of open spaces), but there are hundreds more such as fear of birds, fear of heights, fear of crowds, fear of flying and so on.

Just like phobias, compulsions are restrictive to the person who suffers from them. Here, tension is released by repeating a particular activity again and again such as switching off the lights or locking the doors or turning off the gas on the cooker. The person will, for example, switch off the lights in the house, but then return several times to check again whether all the lights are really off, and they cannot stop themselves from doing this even though they realise they have checked several times already.

Obsessional people carry out activities compulsively, but the obsessive act has a ritualistic component to it. It is almost as if the person is trying to appease an irate god about something the person (subconsciously) feels guilty about. Obsessionals will very methodically arrange all the items on their mantelpiece in a straight line, or feel compelled to count the tiles in the bathroom before they can go to the toilet, or wash their hands an inordinate number of times a day. The longer the routines go on, the more complicated they tend to get, until they control the person's entire life.

All these symptons are indications that the person suffers from something inside himself which is outside his control, and that is where expert help is required. It is important to find the cause that made the symptom necessary in the first place, because every symptom, ludicrous as it may appear to outsiders, has a function, such as keeping excessive fears and feelings of guilt at bay. Once the cause has been discovered and brought to conscious awareness, there is no longer a need for the symptom and it disappears. In order to get to the root-cause of the symptom, I take clients through psychoanalysis under hypnosis in the course of which the client goes over memories of the past. With the help of free association, dream analysis and other techniques, subconscious material is brought to the surface, and eventually repressions emerge that can then be worked through and dealt with consciously.

We tend to greatly underestimate the emotional impact past events have on us, especially when those events occurred in childhood. When we look at the incident with adult eyes, we tend to dismiss it as trivial, but that same incident appears quite different when observed from a child's point of view. Let me give you a few examples.

STAMMERING

A 28-year-old man came to see me for a severe speech impediment. Andrew's stammer was so bad that his whole face contorted with the effort of getting the words out; and yet, despite his disability, he came across as a charismatic person, intelligent and with a great sense of humour. He worked as a civil servant in a position where he had limited contact with the public. He was popular with his colleagues and had managed to build up an efficient support system to help him with his speech impediment. His colleagues would answer his phone for him and he only had to answer occasional enquiries by visitors which he managed to do, albeit with difficulty.

Andrew had tried speech therapy and various other methods over the years, but nothing had brought relief from his problem. As far as he could remember he had always had this stammer.

The first amazing thing happened when he had gone into a relaxed state under hypnosis: he immediately started to speak clearly and fluently, without the slightest hitch, and this continued throughout the ten sessions he came to see me. The moment he was in hypnosis, the speech impediment disappeared completely. This relaxed state would carry on over a short time after the session, but invariably the stammer would return, initially after a few hours, and later after a few days. Relaxation was obviously one aspect that needed to be achieved, but where had the tension come from in the first place?

Andrew's history revealed that he still lived at home with his parents and that he got on well with his mother but had problems with his father whom he described as bad-tempered and dictatorial.

Andrew turned out to be an excellent hypnotic subject with unusually good recall for past events. Not only did be remember easily, but he could also describe smells, tactile sensations and visual images in great detail. As his recall was so extraordinary (which is not the case with every client), I decided to ask him directly rather than wait until free association brought him to the repressed material. I asked him to regress to the time immediately before his stammer started and he spontaneously went back to the age of about three, remembering the following:

He was standing in his garden in front of a flower bed with lots of yellow flowers in it. He knew that his mother liked flowers, so he decided to bring her one. He went and picked one of the yellow flowers, feeling happy and excited about the prospect of pleasing his mother. He turned around to run up the garden path back to the house when he was stopped in his tracks by his father who barred his way, shouted at him at the top of his voice for having picked a flower from the garden, and then smacked him hard 'on the calf of my left leg; I can feel it burning up to my knee right now!' This was the first and last time his father ever smacked him. The little boy's surprise and shock at this sudden attack was so great that he started running back to the house in sheer panic, into the arms of his mother who had come out to see what the noise was all about. She picked him up as he was crying very hard, and as he was sitting on her arm he recalled his mother telling his father off for his harshness ('He's only a baby!') and feeling guilty that he had caused the parents' row.

His mother took him inside into the kitchen, sat him on the draining board by the sink and started wiping his face with a wet cloth. Andrew was still sobbing very hard, at the same time trying to tell his mother what had happened. As he could not breathe properly because he was so upset, his words came out as a stammer, and that was the way it was to remain whenever he was trying to speak.

When I had brought my client out of hypnosis, his first words were, 'I don't believe I just said all that!' All these years, he had totally forgotten about this incident, and yet it had come back so vividly when he remembered that crucial time in his life.

A few more sessions were needed to alleviate the fear of answering the phone. As he had always avoided this task, he lacked experience and felt anxious whenever he had to do it. Apart from occasional hiccups, the stammer was gone, and the last thing I heard from my client was that he had started applying for a new job. With his speech impediment gone, life had suddenly opened up to him with a vast number of new options.

Discussion: This was a very obvious case where personal development had been radically blocked by an event in the past. Had I known about the cause of his stammer and told

Andrew that it was all due to a slap on his leg, he would have found it hard to believe. How could a trivial little incident have so serious an effect? Millions of children get smacked harder and more often and don't start stammering! But it isn't really just the act of slapping the child, it is also the child's individual personality and the way it interprets the smack, as well as the time, place and circumstances why the punishment occurred that have a bearing on the outcome.

PHOBIA

Richard came to see me because of a phobia that threatened to severely restrict his social and professional life. He was a married man with grown-up children and worked as operations manager for a large company. Ever since the age of eight he had had a fear of embarrassing himself in public and of seeing people staring at him and finding him ridiculous. He could not even say what action of his might provoke such an awkward situation, but he felt unable to go to restaurants, theatres or even supermarkets for fear of becoming the focus of attention.

At work, he found it increasingly difficult to sit in meetings, and he would always make sure that he was near a door. When he was asked a question and he felt people looking at him in expectation of his reply, he could just about manage to get a sentence out before he blushed and dried up. The feelings of tightness in the chest would then become so severe that he had to make an excuse and leave the room. Even though he was theoretically perfectly capable of giving a competent answer, his phobia prevented him from doing so.

As his workload had become particularly heavy and domestic problems occurred at the same time, his phobia became worse. He finally decided to seek professional help. He had been off work for two weeks and was afraid of losing his job unless he could get rid of his anxiety soon.

He could trace his fear back to the age of eight when he failed to pass the entrance exam to grammar school. His mother who came from a working class background had had high plans for him and wanted him to join the local rugby club, get into the 'right' kind of school and become a 'gentleman', so when he found out he had failed his exam, he knew that he had also failed his mother.

When he started going out with girls, his phobia started to manifest itself quite clearly. Although he liked one particular girl very much, he felt unable to go to a dance with her. He had taken her all the way to the dance hall in a specially rented car, and then felt unable to take her inside. This made him feel incompetent and a failure and eroded his self-confidence even further.

Over the following years, the fear of embarrassing himself in public grew stronger so that he deliberately started avoiding any situations that could trigger off the phobia. But that was not always possible, and when he was addressed or asked a question in front of other people, he got into such a state that he didn't hear half the question and afterwards felt a profound sense of self-loathing and self-contempt for his weakness. He felt he was continuously pretending and acting as someone he was not.

To prove that he was not altogether useless he kept doing IQ tests and entrance tests for various courses all of which he passed easily, but then he lost interest in the subject. It was as if he was trying to make up for the one test he hadn't passed when he was eight. As he remembered results day at school, the link between his phobia and that particular day finally became clear. He had been confident of having done well in the entrance exam for grammar school and was sitting in class, listening to the teacher reading out the names of the pupils that had passed, when he suddenly realised that his name was not on the list. The teacher continued to say that he was now going to name those pupils who 'have let us down'. One of them was a classmate Richard detested, and the other one was himself.

He remembered how he felt numb with shock at this announcement and dreadfully ashamed and embarrassed for his failure which the teacher had publicly announced in front of all his classmates.

Once this recollection had been worked through and his self-confidence built up, Richard was free of his phobia and began to feel at ease in meetings. He reported that he had been to a restaurant with his daughter and had thoroughly enjoyed the food and the pleasant atmosphere. He had felt quite comfortable and had even had a leisurely drink at the bar while he was waiting for his daughter to arrive.

It took 12 sessions of analytical hypnotherapy to reach that result.

Discussion: In this case, the traumatic incident in childhood had been carried over into later life in a very similar way to the original trigger situation. Even though the client had consciously remembered the incident, it obviously had not been worked through properly at the time. As he had been too shocked at the time to show any emotion and as no attempt was made at home to console him or discuss the issue of having failed the exam with him, he had bottled up all the emotions of guilt, shame and embarrassment, and it was only when he remembered the incident under hypnosis that these emotions finally came out, together with floods of tears. This abreaction released the subconscious pressure which had been causing the phobia over all those years, and once the pressure had gone, the phobia went with it.

By finding the cause and working through it, symptoms are usually made redundant.

IMPOTENCE

Frank was a young man of 23 who was a successful salesman and had never had any problems attracting girls. He was well-groomed and quite aware of his good looks but was getting impatient with himself for his unsatisfactory sexual performance. This seemed the only area in his life where he failed constantly, and this worried him. He had started going out with a girl but had been unable to make love to her because he would either not achieve an erection at all, or the erection was not strong enough for penetration. The only way he could achieve a full erection was by exposing himself on the bus which he had started doing regularly. He talked about this quite openly and did not seem to have any qualms about his unusual behaviour.

Under hypnosis he went over a memory of being touched up by a man on a bus which had led to an erection. He had felt confused and had pushed away the man's hand. This stopped the man for a moment, but then he tried to do it again. This incident occurred when Frank was 17, and it was after this event that he had started exposing himself on buses. However, this memory was not sufficient to explain his inability to achieve an erection when he was in a normal sexual situation with his girlfriend.

I took him back further in time, going over memories of homelife and his parents. He remembered various instances where he was fooling around with boys in his class, but being quite aware that he was really sexually attracted to girls rather than boys. He preferred plump girls, their plumpness reminding him of his mother who he found attractive.

Several memories came up concerning his mother's involvement with other men. One in particular was when he was in bed with his mother and a man who was not his father came into the room. The mother told Frank to go to sleep and the man got into bed and they started making love. On recalling this episode, Frank felt a great sense of sadness, and his voice trailed off into a whisper. Remembering the movement of the duvet he was wondering why his mother was doing this and that it wasn't a very nice thing to happen, expecially not when he was in bed with her. He had always liked sleeping with his mother and nothing had ever happened between them, although he had often indulged in thoughts of penetrating his mother – and now another man was doing this.

After that particular session, Frank felt very dejected and unhappy and left my practice in low spirits. On recollecting these old memories he felt as he had felt then. He was going to see his girlfriend that weekend and did not feel particularly confident about his sexual ability.

When he returned for his next session, however, his mood had changed considerably: he had made love to his girlfriend successfully four times without any problems. Abreacting the upsetting event with his mother and her lover had removed the block that had prevented him from engaging in successful love-making.

It took Frank five sessions of analysis to deal with his past and overcome his problem of impotence.

Discussion: Sexual problems often go back to events that have sexual connotations. Impotence or frigidity can be caused by having been subjected to forced sexual practices as a child or teenager, or it can be brought about by witnessing sexual acts being carried out by others. Children often find it hard to understand what is going on when they become aware of their own sexuality, and more often than not, the urge to masturbate or any sexual fantasies are accompanied by feelings of guilt, especially when these fantasies concern their own mother.

Just as in Steven's case (see below), Frank felt a sense of anger at his mother for betraying him and his father with someone else, but Frank could never let that feeling of anger show because he himself felt guilty for having sexual thoughts concerning his mother.

Even though all these confused feelings were repressed into the subconscious of his mind, they still had an effect on his emotional equilibrium. As sex is entirely dependent on balanced emotions, Frank's inability to make love could not be overcome until past emotional blockage was removed.

More often than not, a block goes back not to one isolated incident but to a series of episodes that reflect the prevailing (negative) atmosphere at the time.

DEPRESSION

Steven came to see me originally to stop smoking. He was on 80 cigarettes a day and beginning to get really worried about his habit which he was unable to get under control, let alone break. He described himself as severely depressed and suffering from total lack of self-confidence and self-esteem. Although he was strikingly handsome he hated his looks and, above all, himself. It was obvious that his smoking habit was masking some far more serious underlying problem, so rather than giving him suggestions to stop smoking, we agreed on analytical treatment to 'tidy up' the past.

His memories were of great loneliness, humiliation and repeated rejection. His mother was cold towards him and seemed to regard it as a chore having to look after a child, making him feel he was messy and always in the way. She condemned and criticised him constantly, calling him stupid, and nothing he did could please her. He felt he was a nobody. His father, though kindlier, was weak and unable to stand up to the domineering mother who would deceive her husband with other men. Steven remembered being taken along to one of her rendezvous at the age of four, sitting in a car on his mother's lap while she was talking to a strange man who she seemed to be close to. He remembered feeling betrayed by his mother, sensing that she was doing something wrong against him and his father.

Because his parents travelled a lot he was put into boarding school where he was mercilessly bullied and hit by other boys. Although it was not pleasant at home, school was even worse, so every time he had to go back he started screaming and yelling and got totally hysterical. He was consequently severely punished by his mother who never asked *why* he didn't want to go back; it was just assumed that he was being difficult and making a big fuss over nothing. He was threatened with further punishment unless he stopped his unreasonable behaviour and dragged back to school.

In order to get away from humiliation and criticism, the child began to withdraw and became a loner. He would be happiest when he was on his own, escaping human company wherever he could. But even that was punished. One day his parents took him along to an adult party where there were no other children. As he was left to his own devices, he wandered off into a nearby derelict building to play. When his parents found him there, they took him back and locked him in the boot of their car as punishment.

By this time, the message had been firmly implanted in his mind that he was unlikeable, stupid and worthless.

During his sessions, all the despair and sadness about his situation came out, but also a lot of anger; anger and contempt for his father who, although kinder than his mother, had never helped or defended him or cared enough for his son to spend time with him and who had not had the guts to do something about his wife's blatant infidelities, and even greater anger at his mother who had treated him in such a contemptible and cruel manner. As the anger came out, the depression began to lift and Steven began to get a new perspective. What his mother had referred to as stupidity in him he recognised as having been disinterest, realising that academic subjects he felt attracted to he mastered very well. He also came to understand that he was justified in being angry at the treatment that he had received, and if his mother had been wrong in the way she had behaved towards him then she could also have been wrong in what she had said about him. She had misjudged him and consequently he was misjudging his own abilities now. This insight came as a great relief. Within a few sessions the depression had gone altogether and the client felt that 'the real person' was now able to come out of the shell. By the last session but one he had cut down to 20 cigarettes a day, and by the last session he had stopped smoking altogether.

He has since begun to revise his circle of friends and gone about rearranging his life which includes leaving a job he never wanted to do and going on a course to study art.

Discussion: This case was unusual in that it took only nine sessions to bring it to a conclusion and turn around suicidal despair into new hope and a sense of being in control of life once again. It is encouraging to see how years of misery and their detrimental effects can be dealt with and resolved to allow a person to free their true potential.

It does not mean that Steven has now left all difficulties behind him, it just means that he is now free to make his own choices. Even though the official analysis is over, the process of gaining insight and finding out things about himself continues, but now he is able to deal with it himself.

Analysis opens the door to let some light into a previously dark room, and once this is done the client is able to push the door open all the way himself.

PRE-MENSTRUAL TENSION (PMT)

A young woman in her mid-thirties, let us call her Laura, consulted me for a number of health problems she had had over many years, the most serious of which were severe mood swings two weeks prior to her period when she was oscillating between phases of tearfulness and irritability, hyperactivity and lethargy. She suffered from sleeping problems and, in spite of bronchitis, she could not bring herself to stop smoking. No organic cause was found for these health problems, so a psychosomatic origin had to be considered.

Laura was the younger of two girls. Although she adored her father, it was her older sister Jane who was the father's favourite, given privileges and generally treated more leniently. The mother appeared to favour the older daughter, too. Whenever anything went wrong, it was automatically Laura who was blamed.

She went to a very strict convent school where the girls were caned for any misbehaviour. Once, Laura spoke to her neighbour in class because she hadn't understood what the teacher was saying, and without even being asked why she had talked, she was punished. She particularly remembered one of the nuns as being exceptionally vicious; it appeared that she enjoyed punishing the children and would do so for the smallest of reasons. If ever her mother found out that she had been punished at school, she would often also reprimand or beat Laura when she got home without allowing her to explain what had happened. However, the worst thing was that the mother would then tell the father about Laura's alleged misdemeanours, whereupon he showed disappointment and anger at his daughter's failings. It appeared that Laura could not please anyone, no matter how hard she tried. Whatever she did was never good enough, and any naughtiness or blunder was immediately counted against her and used to confirm the general opinion that Laura was simply 'no good'.

Her older sister bullied her mercilessly, putting her down in front of friends and frightening her whenever she could. She would make fun of her wetting the bed and even go as far as embarrassing her in front of visitors by showing them the soaked mattress. As the parents always took Jane's side, there was no one to turn to, and it seemed as if everybody was closing ranks against her, making her feel unwanted and like an outsider.

When the father died, the family moved in with the maternal grandmother for a while but had to move out after a row. They then set up house in a large city where the mother rented rooms. As the money was needed desperately and as there were not enough rooms for both the children and the lodgers, Laura was made to share her room with a 22-year-old lodger, Robert. She was 14 years old at the time. Eventually, Robert persuaded her to sleep with him, although she felt it was wrong. However, as she had to share the room with him, she could not evade his persistent advances, so she finally gave in to him. The relationship continued over the following three years.

Her mother had in the meantime started a relationship with Simon, another young lodger, who stayed with her in her bedroom at nights. One day, the mother decided to alter arrangements. She told Laura suddenly that it was wrong for her to share a bedroom with a man at her age and asked her to sleep in her, the mother's, bedroom from now on. Laura did not like the idea as she was aware that her mother's boyfriend was going to be there as well. Laura was not allowed to come into the bedroom until everyone else was in bed. Once she was in bed in her mother's bedroom, she tried to go to sleep as quickly as possible, but often could not help overhearing her mother and the boyfriend making love.

If she got tired before everyone else was in bed, she had to make her bed in the sitting room which was also rented to a male lodger, and try to go to sleep which she often found impossible because the lodger had the television on and refused to turn it down for her. When the girl told her mother that she could not go to sleep, the mother dismissed her complaints by telling her not to make a fuss: the lodger would soon go to sleep.

One Christmas, Laura caught her mother kissing Robert, Laura's boyfriend. When she started screaming at her mother, the mother told her she was just jealous and had only imagined it, and anyway, it had only been a Christmas kiss. Laura asked her mother why she didn't kiss Robert in front of her if it was so harmless, and the mother replied that she hadn't done so because of Laura's unreasonable jealousy.

It appeared that, again, Laura was losing out. Whenever she had achieved something or formed a relationship, her mother or her sister would spoil it for her. It seemed that whatever she did was wrong and whatever she owned she would lose eventually.

Laura tried to commit suicide twice. After the second time she was referred to a psychiatrist who was to clarify the reasons for her depression. Instead, he touched her up under the pretext of giving her a physical examination to see whether she had been sexually abused. Laura was highly distressed but did not dare speak to her mother or anyone else about this, for fear of being told off and accused of having invented it.

Discussion: Under hypnosis, all the above memories came flooding back, accompanied by emotions of anger, distress, shame and grief. Several of the incidents, as for example the one with the psychiatrist, had been repressed and emerged, much to Laura's surprise, during her sessions of hypnoanalysis.

Once the repressions were released, Laura's sleep pattern became normal again and she noticed how her mood became more positive and stable; her PMT had gone. Remembering and working through the traumatic events in her past, her self-esteem started improving and she could stop blaming herself for all the things that had gone wrong in her life. She also began to cut down on her smoking. Analysis was completed in 6 sessions.

Although in many cases the circumstances are not as severe as those described here, I have often come across a distinct psychological basis for PMT.

Finally, I would like to give a further couple of examples of how development can be blocked by something in the past, but in these cases, the trigger event occurred not during childhood but during a period later in life.

Overweight

A lady in her mid-forties came to see me with a serious weight problem. Christine was married for the second time, had four children and had found it impossible to stop over-eating ever since she had got married to her second husband. She was four stone overweight and close to despair. She had tried all sorts of diets with varying degrees of success, and although she had managed to stick to some of the diets and lose a stone or two, the moment she stopped the diet she put all the weight on again. By the time she came to see me she had nearly given up, but one of her friends who had been to see me for overweight and had successfully lost her excess pounds suggested she give hypnotherapy a try.

Christine had got married at 18 because she was pregnant, and the first years of marriage went well until her husband grew distant and stayed away from home more and more. When he came home, he would be silent and not offer any explanation as to where he had been. Christine finally found out that he had started an affair with a woman he had met at work, a divorcee ten years his senior. Over the following years, there were fights and tears because he refused to end the affair, and finally he told Christine that he had lost interest in her and was going to leave her for his mistress.

She was devastated. He moved out of the marital home, leaving her with two little children – and pregnant with a third as she found out two weeks after he had left. She rang him at work to tell him, hoping that this would entice him to come home. Instead, he made it clear that he had no intention of returning to her or paying for another child which he insinuated was not his anyway. The young

woman saw no other way but to have the pregnancy ter-
minated.

She borrowed the money and booked herself into a clinic
although she was strongly opposed to abortion. She was
horrified to see young girls, casually admitting that this
was their second or third termination, when she felt so
wrong about getting rid of her baby but felt she had no
other option because of her desperate situation.

All this came out under hypnosis ten years later, together
with the feelings of guilt and shame and utter self-hate for
what she had done. She had been unable to talk to anyone
about the abortion, least of all her family who were strict
Roman Catholics.

Shortly after the abortion, she met her second husband.
At the same time, she started divorce proceedings against
her first husband which turned out to be very antagonistic.
She began to overeat, attributing this to the stressful financial situation she was in due to her husband's refusal to
pay maintenance for her and the children.

Once the repressed feelings about the abortion came out,
however, her eating habits changed radically. She reported
that she felt a lot better within herself and didn't feel the
need to comfort-eat any more. Also, her self-confidence
had increased and she would no longer allow other people
to push her around as she used to do out of a feeling of self-
loathing. When she finished her analysis she had already
started losing weight, and the last I have heard of her is
that she had nearly reached her target weight.

Discussion: We can see here how unresolved guilt can have
a serious effect on all sorts of behavioural aspects. Feelings
of guilt and remorse lead to inner conflict, and behaviour
tends to become self-punishing, as if to say, 'I've done
wrong. I'm not worth looking at, I might as well stuff
myself.' With this client, the feelings of guilt also resulted
in an attitude of being inferior because of what she had
done, and because she behaved like an underdog, she was
unable to command respect from others.

After having gone through analysis, she still felt that it
was wrong to terminate a pregnancy, but she could now
see that with the pressure she had been under at the time,

she had been unable to find an alternative solution; in other words, she learned to forgive herself, and this opened the way to new behaviours and a changed attitude towards herself.

I have dealt with countless cases where women claimed that the abortion they had had years ago hadn't affected them – only to cry their eyes out under analysis as they went over the memory again, much to their own surprise. Consciously we can rationalise our doubts, fears and guilt away, but subconsciously these feelings still remain, and unless we deal with them, they will act as a block that hinders our progress in life.

STRESS

Adam was working for a newspaper in a highly pressured job which required a constant working towards deadlines and high-level performance in a fast-moving environment. Not surprisingly, things would go wrong every once in a while and people would make mistakes which unfortunately always resulted in a witchhunt to find the 'culprit'.

Adam had suffered from anxiety for several years when he came to see me. Even though he knew he was good at his job he felt highly distressed at the rankling and scheming that was going on, always afraid of being not at his best and consequently the target of a scapegoating campaign. He was dissatisfied with the fact that he was given his boss's work to do whenever she was away from the office or on holiday. His own workload was heavy enough as it was, and any extra work resulted in an overload situation which made errors and mistakes more likely. However, he felt unable to voice his discontent because he abhorred arguments. Adam had been prescribed tranquilizers for his anxiety which he took only when the anxiety got out of hand.

Adam had been a sensitive child who did well at school and had lots of friends. He did not go on to university because of financial problems at home. He met his wife when he was 18 and married young. They later had a son.

The marriage was good and he enjoyed being with his family.

As he was going through his past under hypnosis, he remembered various events in his childhood and adolescence that explained his fear of arguments. His father had suffered from diabetes but had refused to take insulin or keep to a diet, and as a consequence, had suffered from mood swings. Adam remembered numerous rows between his parents during mealtimes. His mother always seemed to lose these arguments against his father who tended to get verbally aggressive. Sometimes the rows would escalate to such an extent that Adam had to leave the room because he was so upset.

The father had been a bit of a loner who kept himself to himself but liked to be seen as the head of the family. He had his views on things and was not prepared to deviate from them, always pointing out that he knew what was best for his wife and children. When Adam started developing his own political views and began to voice them in school essays, his father became annoyed with him and started verbally attacking him for his different opinion. Since the father's shouting intimidated Adam, he always ended up backing off.

In spite of their differences, Adam liked his father, so it came as a shock to him when his father suddenly died, two months before Adam's wedding. The father had been rushed into hospital unexpectedly one day. Adam had returned from work in the evening when he received a phone call from the hospital to come over immediately because his father was in a critical condition. He and his mother rushed to the hospital, but his father had died by the time they got there.

Adam felt angry at his father. Why hadn't he taken insulin? Was he so unhappy that he wanted to die? Adam felt that it had been selfish of his father to refuse medication, thus accelerating his ill health and cutting down on the time he could have spent with Adam.

As his mother was too distressed, it was up to Adam to sort out the funeral arrangements. As everything had happened so suddenly, there was no time for tears and grieving, because as soon as the funeral was over, Adam had to see to the arrangements for his own wedding a few weeks later. The contrast was bizarre: on his wedding day he was expected to be happy and light-hearted, and he himself wanted to enjoy the day, but his father's death was still too fresh in his mind; he felt torn between two extremes.

Under hypnosis, Adam was able to release the grief about his father's death which he had been unable to experience at the time. Looking after his distressed mother and sorting out funeral arrangements as well as his own guilt-inducing feelings of anger towards his father had prevented him from grieving, and his own wedding shortly afterwards had cut short the mourning period. Going over these events that occurred when he was 20 years old brought all the emotional components back that had been present at the time but had remained unexpressed. Abreacting these feelings came as a great relief to Adam, and he felt that an important thing had finally been set right.

He was later able to develop a new attitude towards arguments and eventually succeeded in making his own wishes known at work without feeling guilty or too hampered by anxiety.

Discussion: This is another example of how an event later on in life can have a prfound effect on a person's ability to progress in life.

Adam had come to fear arguments because they had made him feel helpless and anxious when he was a child. As his father's way of arguing was an aggressive one it scared him and Adam started to avoid getting involved in any issues that might cause dissent, thus trying to prevent anxiety from arising.

This avoidance strategy worked to a certain extent, but it also had its drawbacks. Although Adam would not voice his dissent he still felt anger and resentment, both at work and in various episodes with his father. As he was a timid person he tried to avoid inflicting unpleasantness onto others, so he repressed those negative feelings, but this only resulted in his developing anxieties that threatened to take over his life.

Unexpressed feelings led to emotional stress, and his

father's death with all the unwelcome and seemingly inappropriate feelings marked the epitome of repression which needed to be released in order to make new attitudes and new ways of behaviour possible.

16. CONCLUSION

THERE are many ways of finding happiness and fulfilment in life, as many ways as there are people.

This book is meant to give you insight into the reasons and causes that can block you and prevent you from progressing to reach your full potential, and I have attempted to give you ideas and practical advice on how to select and pursue your own personal aims and achieve personal growth.

There is one step, however, this book cannot make for you, and that is to go out there and do it. The book can show you the way, but you will have to walk down the road yourself.

The only person who really knows what you need is *you*; the only person who knows what is best for you is *you*; and the only person who can make you happy is *you*, and this means that it is *you* who is responsible to see to it that you strive to become the best possible person.

Start working on it NOW – it is worth it!

INDEX